THE INCOMPARABLE LADY

YO-FEI AND HIS MISSUS IN VIENNA

THE INCOMPARABLE LADY

Tributes and Other Memorabilia Pertaining to

FLORENCE WHEELOCK AYSCOUGH MacNAIR

Compiled and Edited by HARLEY FARNSWORTH MacNAIR

PRIVATELY PRINTED AT CHICAGO · 1946

" . . . . *and we have made a vow to learn*
of her from all who have so much as seen
her. In that way, little by little we will
learn the truth about her, the lovely truth
about her who was loveliness itself. . . . .

. . . . *In her small body were the seeds*
of dream, as potent after as before its
death. They blow still across the moun-
tains and deserts of the East, as thistle-
down dreams of Helen still drift from
the Western Sea.

What was Helen; what was Yang Kuei-fei?
What, for that matter, is anyone, until
the thought of him takes root, and flowers
to the colour of the mind that feeds it?

—MAUDE MEAGHER, *White Jade* (Boston
and New York, 1930), pp. 4 and xii.

For the pleasure
Of
A few of many
Who know
(That is, love—since to know is to love)

FLORENCE WHEELOCK AYSCOUGH MACNAIR

Whether personally, or through her lectures
And other deeds in many lands
Or through her correspondence and published works
In which joyously and colorfully while on this plane
She expressed her personality
            And
Unconsciously wrought an autobiography
            But
        Most of all
        For Myself
    Who know her best
        And therefore
Do most reverence and adore her

FOREWORD

Now that I have read the proofs, and the time has come finally to separate this small book from myself, I realize more keenly than before, if that be possible, the utter inadequacy of my attempts to portray, in part, the personality of The Incomparable Lady. None could do her justice—I, who should most nearly be able to, least of all. Accordingly, I am more grateful even than during the months preceding and following her departure for the tributes to her contained in the hundreds of letters sent to us during that period. Many of these are so beautiful, and reflect so clearly a few of the facets of her character, that they merit reading by others than those who composed and those who received them. Her friends needed not to write with restraint or to fear charges of sentimentality. I, to whom she means most, cannot write without restraint—and, what the Chinese call, the "controlled brush," or pen, depicts but a part of the truth, and that stiffly and with little charm.

I wish to thank all who, directly and indirectly and unwittingly, have contributed to this collection. I have asked permission from no one to make use of what is here incorporated—but if I had not been appreciative of their "contributions," what is here included would not have been chosen. I am equally appreciative of the very considerable number of eulogies which lack of space prevented printing.

Directly, I wish to thank the University of Chicago Press for making possible the appearance of this volume at a time when the making of books is unusually difficult. Particularly do I thank Miss Alice Brown for her contribution to a most important part of this record, and Miss Mary D. Alexander and Mr. Herman Bauman for their advice and other aid with respect to the composition of the book.

Last of all—but very far from least—I thank, by the printed word, the distinguished Canadian-American artist, Nan Rice, for the remarkable portrait, which she made this summer, of The Incomparable Lady.

H. F. M.

THE HOUSE OF THE WU-T'UNG TREES
September 26, 1946

CONTENTS

PART I

POIGNANT GRIEF DURING A SUNNY SPRING

By LI T'AI-PO

THE East wind has come again.
I see the jade-green grass and realize that it is Spring.
Everywhere there is an immense confusion of ripples and
  agitations.
Why does the waving and fluttering of the weeping-willow make
  me sad?
The sky is so bright it shines; everything is lovely and at
  peace.
The breath of the sea is green, fresh, sweet-smelling;
The heaths are vari-coloured, blue—green—as a kingfisher
  feather. Oh-h-h-h-h—How far one can see!
Clouds whirl, fly, float, and cluster together, each one sharply
  defined;
Waves are smoothed into a wide, continuous flowing.
I examine the young moss in the well, how it starts into
  life.
I see something dim—Oh-h-h-h-h—waving up and down
  like floss silk.
I see it floating—it is a cobweb, coiling like smoke.
Before all these things—Oh-h-h-h-h—my soul is severed
  from my body.
Confronted with the wind, the brilliance, I suffer.

(1)

I feel as one feels listening to the sound of the waters of the
    Dragon Mound in Ch'in,
The gibbons wailing by the Serpent River.
I feel as the "Shining One" felt when she passed the Jade
    Frontier,
As the exile of Ch'u in the Maple Forest.
I will try to climb a high hill and look far away into the
    distance.
Pain cuts me to the bone and wounds my heart.
My Spring heart is agitated as the surface of the sea,
My Spring grief is bewildered like a flurry of snow.
Ten thousand emotions are mingled—their sorrow and their
    joy.
Yet I know only that my heart is torn in this Spring season.
She of whom I am thinking—Oh-h-h-h-h—is at the shore
    of the Hsiang River,
Separated by the clouds and the rainbow—without these
    mists I could surely see.
I scatter my tears a foot's length upon the water's surface.
I entrust the Easterly flowing water with my passion for the
    Cherished One.
If I could command the shining of the Spring, could grasp it
    without putting it out—Oh-h-h-h-h—
I should wish to send it as a gift to that beautiful person at the
    border of Heaven.

                        —*Fir-Flower Tablets*, pp. 32–33.

(2)

TO MRS. HOLLIS WILBUR

My dear Mrs. Wilbur:

Often and often since you and others asked me to write a life of Florence, I have pondered your request. You are correct, I think, in your suggestion that no one *knew* Florence, as she was on this plane, and appreciated the beauty of her character and personality and the greatness and many-sidedness of her ability as did I. But more than comprehension and adoration are necessary to the composition of a memoir worthy of such a being. As I have waited, it has been made increasingly clear that if your suggestion is ever to be carried out, it must be by one who can write not alone with knowledge and affection but with detachment, serenity, *and* a distinguished style. In the three last-mentioned qualifications I am lacking.

History and literature demonstrate that distinction of style is primarily a matter of genius; only secondarily is it one of training and experience. Florence was qualified by both genius and experience to have composed an outstanding formal autobiography; informally, she did this in her books and correspondence. She was not, however, sufficient of an egotist to take time from Chinese literature, United China Relief, the American Friends of China, and other activities to write of herself—as, time and again, I begged her to do.

For some individuals (if one may judge by their biographies) all that is considered necessary is a pedestrianly factual account: they were born, they lived, they died. In some cases, doubtless, this is all that is merited, possibly more. In others, it would appear that the subjects deserved more from their biographers than they received. With respect to Florence, I am determined that, in so far as I am concerned, her brightness shall not be tarnished by the publication of an inadequate biography. To be sure, the whole cannot be greater than its parts, but if the parts are not seen in focus, and if they are not properly integrated, the whole —or what purports to be the whole—may appear to be considerably less than its parts. In no field of knowledge is this more commonly demonstrated than in the biographical.

Florence was a very great person—not, primarily, because of what she did but because of what she was. The Chinese saying, "Heaven does not tolerate perfection"—so often quoted by her—to the contrary notwithstanding, her character was perfectly balanced and rounded. Her personality was exquisite. There was nothing one-sided about her: outdoor life and sports she enjoyed as greatly as indoor studies; her hands she used as she did her mind, in perfect co-ordination. The results of one type of work gave her as deep a satisfaction as those of the other. Remarking often, "What man has done, man [especially woman!] can do," she was as practical as she was aesthetic. This was shown time and again ten years ago this spring when we were making changes prior to occupying what we named "The House of the Wu-t'ung Trees." The wu-t'ung, you will remember, is the only tree, according to Chinese mythology, on which the Bird of Happiness rests. As long as she was here, the Bird of Happiness not only alighted upon but made its home in the two wu-t'ungs by our door.

Florence it was, and not the consulting architect or the contractor, who solved one particularly difficult problem—that of *making* space for a lavatory on the main floor. She studied the original plans for the house, noted the arrangements of the pipes, and evolved "The Finger Bowl"—suitable for what British Museum authorities once referred to as "casual ablutions" and for the changing of the mind, if not the raiment, of anyone not of elephantine proportions.

When, during the same period of joyful stress, I suggested the removal of a partition to enlarge the living-room, Florence agreed—but, more farsighted than Lady Macbeth, queried, "*How* many pipes, do you suppose, are in that wall?" It was as full of pipes as Duncan's body was of blood. Removal of the partition, and its contents, resulted in giving the new room two large doorways into the hall which were only four feet apart.

"We'll plaster up the old entrance," said I. "We certainly do not want *two* doorways 'side by each.'"

"No," replied Florence, "we'll keep *both* entrances. When there are large groups passing between the library and the draw-

ing-room, we don't want jams in the doorway. With two open-
ings, guests can move around without stepping on each other.
We'll have a plywood partition for the larger entrance, paper it
like the rest of the room, cover it with a tapestry or with paintings—and remove it easily when necessary." Thus it was done,
and the first reception vindicated her judgment.

Of the truly innumerable charms of her completely untempera-
mental personality (in addition to the depth and breadth and
scintillation of her mind), her beauty and gracious kindliness
and boundless sympathy, her creative imagination and consequent tolerance, and her whimsical humor and delightfully
absurd "good-luck" superstitions were outstanding. (*Never*
would she admit to a belief in "*bad*-luck" superstitions.) The
sight in Europe of a chimneysweep, or anywhere, when we were
motoring, of a load of hay, or of a flock of sheep on the *left* side
of the road or of pigs on the *right*, filled her with joy. But if I
pointed to sheep on the right, or to pigs on the left, she would
studiously gaze in the opposite direction—and declare that *she*
saw no such animals *any*where. When the new moon appeared, she
would invite me to accompany her outdoors to bow to it nine
times, and on New Year's Eve she would mount a stool just before midnight so as to "jump into the New Year" on the stroke
of the hour.

Florence was, in all senses of the word "beauty," the most
beautiful person I have ever known. From that bright autumnal
afternoon in 1916, when she opened the door of the library in
the old Royal Asiatic Society building on Museum Road, crossed
the room to me (I was using the card catalogue), and said in
that exquisite voice, "Good afternoon! I am Mrs. Ayscough; can
I help you in any way?" and added, "I am Honorary Librarian
of the R.A.S.," I have loved her. In the course of our first conversation on my work at St. John's University, and her interest
in the R.A.S., on that doubly bright afternoon (I can still smell
the musty odor of the old books in that room, so characteristic
of Shanghai), she declared: "You must come to tea with me
soon; I will write you to fix the day."

At this time she was living in Wild Goose Happiness House at
60 Gordon Road, and, after tea before the fireplace in the drawing-room surrounded by her books, we walked in the garden in

which she took so much pleasure and from which came the flowers that won her many prizes in the Shanghai horticultural shows. That afternoon was the first of numberless occasions, during the ensuing nineteen years before our marriage, when, in Shanghai, and later in St. Andrews, Chicago, and Guernsey, we had tea together to discuss Chinese or other history, art, civilization, travel—and *books*.

Of the many pleasures of life in China in those years, the greatest was having tea—on many occasions followed by dinner, since I had so much difficulty in, as Brer Rabbit used to say, "scraping myself off the verandah"—with "Mrs. Ayscough." (It will not surprise you, but it may amuse you, to learn that not until I went to Guernsey to marry her did I use her given name or she mine.) From the moment of receiving an invitation until the afternoon arrived, I looked forward with happiness. Despite my eagerness, however, I was, for some unaccountable reason, careful *never* to arrive even five minutes before the hour set. It was not easy to estimate with precision the ricksha or walking or motor time between St. John's and 60 Gordon Road or, later, 72 Penang Road after she had built The Grass Hut. More than once I strolled around a few minutes before ringing the bell. After our marriage I learned that, in Florence's estimation, the one unpardonable *faux pas* was the arrival of a guest *one* moment *before* the time set. A guest might be half an hour late—that she was accustomed to, living as she had so many years on the outskirts of the International Settlement—but to arrive early was almost unforgivable. Heaven in this matter, as in so many others, was on my side in developing my intuition.

To converse once with Florence was to gain knowledge and inspiration. To converse often was to gain an education, especially with respect to China, and to develop an outlook on life which could never desert one.

Early in our friendship she directed my attention to the value of the writings of Thomas Taylor Meadows and lent me his invaluable *Desultory Notes*. She was generous in lending books but discriminating in her choice of borrowers. Miss Lowell, possibly wisely, would lend to *none;* she might, and apparently often did, if an unenlightened person asked the loan of a volume, purchase a copy and present it—but she would not lend. To a year-round resident of St. Andrews, Florence one autumn contemplated offering the key to her library while she was to be in Europe. Unfortunately, or fortunately—depending upon the viewpoint—this person airily remarked to her, "Oh, a book is like an umbrella—one never dreams of returning either!" The key was not lent.

In contrast to the teas served by most Americans in Shanghai, Florence's afternoon tea was exceedingly simple and not an ostentatiously calorific affair. To you, certainly, I need not comment on the quality of the *tea!* It was accompanied only, but quite sufficiently, by thin slices of buttered bread and thin slices of a simple uniced pound cake. (I shall not forget a time when Mother and I were asked to tea with an acquaintance who apparently believed that the object of tea was physical rather than mental sustenance. There were, as I remember, about five guests. The dining table was loaded with almost everything except ham and eggs. J. B. Powell, coming late, glanced at the table and murmured in my ear as he passed to greet the hostess, "*China,* Land of Famine"!) For Florence, who disliked meat and cared little for food at any hour of the day, tea was an occasion for exchanges of ideas with friends around a fire or in a garden.

During the winter and early spring in Shanghai before our marriage, on the days—fairly numerous—when I was expected, Florence used to inform the Boy: "Today, Dr. MacNair come for tea—other man no can see." In other words, she was "not at home" to accidental callers. This also I learned only after our marriage!

A garden to Florence was something to plan carefully, to work and rest in—and not merely to look at through windows. The walled courts of The Grass Hut, tiny as compared to the spacious lawns of Wild Goose Happiness House, were exquisite in their meticulously careless "natural" arrangement of trees, bamboos, shrubs, a tiny pool with arched bridge, hillocks, and Chinese rockeries. The glory of the garden at St. Andrews, with its flower borders and slightly sloping sweep of grass, was its outlook to the blue-gray waters of Passamaquoddy Bay and the dark forested island (with its overnight log cabin and adjoining fresh-water swimming pool) which were framed in the large window of the drawing-room. At 22 Hauteville, Guernsey, the old, high-walled fruit and flower garden also faces to the—here —emerald-green sea (there are no rivers to muddy the coastal waters) and to the harbor of St. Peter Port, which is divided by a mole connecting the ruins of the medieval castle with the island. Over this garden, to the harbor and the castle and the English Channel, the small living-room, and Florence's bedroom above, faced. In the latter high chamber—the house, approached by a narrow, winding, ancient cobble-stoned street, clings to a hill-side some hundreds of feet above the Lower Town—one seemed, as she wrote me, suspended between sky and sea.

Florence hated to be shut in by either walls or mountains or to be cut off from immediate touch with the earth. Apartment living was not for her. Elemental, she loved the vastness of the sea, with its eternal movement, and wanted to work in the soil, to plant seeds and watch them grow, to put on old clothes, kneel on a mat, and dig weeds from flowerbeds and lawns. In Guernsey she purchased, in L'Erère, le Camp de Varouf, a plot of about an acre, in a thinly populated section across the island from Hauteville and St. Peter Port. There, on an unprotected rocky shore, treeless and facing westward over the Atlantic, she planned to have built a Guernsey-type two-roomed stone cottage on the very edge of the shore so that, when visiting the Channel Islands, she might step into the sea whenever she wanted to swim. The one drawback to the five-storied old stone house with its gay red front door at 22 Hauteville, with its wonderful view to Sark, Jethou, and the coast of France near Cherbourg, was that she had to clamber down half a mile or so to the beach to enjoy a bathe in the sea. I am sure she has chosen for her abode now a wild bit of the Western Paradise where waters roll and winds blow, and where she can swim in a never-ever changing sea. I am equally certain that near by there is a garden in which she can create beauty and converse with Tu Fu, Li Po, and others of the poets whom she loved, and that she has access to a heavenly library in which she can carry on her studies.

You, who have experienced Chicago, can easily imagine my hesitation to bring Florence from the great beauty and quiet cleanliness of Guernsey to the grime and noise of this city. Knowing herself, however, and her ability to make a garden, spiritual and physical, wherever she might be, the one question

(8)

she considered, as she later informed me, was: "*Can* I live in the overheated houses of America?" Her solution, in part, to this problem—in below-freezing weather at times—was to wrap herself warmly and write in the garden outside the library. During the winter in which we lived near Jackson Park, she used also to walk there with me to carry food to the birds and squirrels; subsequently she fed them in our garden here. Her love of animals and humans, her vividness and kindness, reminded me often of St. Francis of Assisi.

When we were shown what became the House of the Wu-t'ung Trees, she was delighted with two in particular of its advantages: there was room for our combined libraries (most of her books had been stored for several years while she "caravaned" on the Continent and, later, while she was living in Guernsey) *and*— there was a garden. That a grassy space with fine trees and shrubbery, and ample opportunity for digging, could be found in a great city filled her with joy, especially after her physically restricted existence in Vienna and London.

From the time Florence first became acquainted with Chicago in 1917, she had considered this city the most stimulating in the United States. It pulsed with life; it was youthfully vigorous in outlook; it faced the future, as did she, with confidence. Vulgarity there was, but vulgarity is of the essence of life, and manifestations of creative imagination and intellectuality accompanied it on every hand. No other city had a "front yard" equaling Chicago's with its magnificent buildings, parks, and drives, supplemented by a body of water unmarred by docks and warehouses—while *many* cities, unfortunately, had "back yards" no less lacking in beauty. Chicago's press-inspired reputation for municipal corruption and gangsters she regretted, but, acquainted with Boston, New York, Shanghai, and the cities of Europe, she did not consider that, in this, Chicago was unique.

Moreover, her Unitarian-based belief[1]—supplemented by her

[1] This belief is well illustrated in the following excerpt from the Litany in an Order of Service in the First Unitarian Church, with which she affiliated herself in Chicago:

MINISTER: O Thou Eternal Light, toward whose quickening dawn have moved the peoples that walked in darkness, rise with thy radiance upon the souls which here await thee.

By the visions of ancient seers who beheld thy power moving within the veil of earthly things;

studies in Chinese thought—in man's limitless potentialities for spiritual elevation and physical and mental development prevented doubt as to humanity's ultimate salvation. Although, like Tu Fu, she could describe herself as being by nature "impatient, *very*," she had also a truly Chinese sense of time—and timelessness.

It may be added, with reference to her religio-philosophical attitudes, that she would not condone weakness, error, or wrong on the ground that, "after all, we are only human." "*Only* human? But humanity is *divine*." Entirely willing to participate, in so far as permitted by the clergy, in the communion and other services of the Episcopal, or Anglican, Church, she would not join in the repetition of the General Confession: "Go down on my knees and tell *God* that I am a 'miserable sinner'? Never! I would not so *insult* the Deity."

The four years that have passed since Florence was promoted to another plane have but added to my devotion to her. Her every move was graceful; her every expression of thought was constructive, positive, and stimulating. Except toward evil, there was no negativity in her. Never, when she was present, was there a dull moment. Unlike some who sparkle mainly abroad, she was more fascinating and amusing and altogether delightful at home than when she was out.

I could never decide—and I meditated often upon it—in what

PEOPLE: *Teach us to live as seeing the invisible.*

MINISTER: By the voices of holy prophets who discerned the signs of their times and foretold the doom that follows wrong;

PEOPLE: *Arouse us to see and overcome the evils of today.*

MINISTER: By the mind that was in Christ Jesus; compassionate, free in thought, steadfast in purpose, stayed on thee;

PEOPLE: *Awaken in us also a generous mind and a bold vision.*

MINISTER: By the sacrifice of saints and apostles, martyrs and missioners who counted not the cost to themselves if they might testify of thy grace;

PEOPLE: *Inspire us to find in common life the paths of high devotion.*

MINISTER: By the joy and praise of thy holy church, by every prayer for light in shrines of whatsoever faith, in east or west or north or south;

PEOPLE: *Kindle in our hearts the faith that shall be a light upon our way and a song upon our lips.*

MINISTER: By the labors of all who show forth thy wonderful works; searching out thy law in nature, fashioning forms of beauty, skilful in industry, wise in statecraft, gentle in parenthood;

PEOPLE: *Enlarge all our being with the fulness of thy divine life, that in thy light we may see light and become ministers of thy love brought near.* AMEN.

proportion her beauty was physical and in what spiritual. The one perfectly matched the other. But this I know: If she had been completely lacking in external beauty, she would still—with her soul, and mind, and voice—have been the loveliest of women. Not until our marriage did I comprehend why the Catholic branches of the Christian Church include marriage among the sacraments.

And not least in the manifestations of her loveliness, and in the exemplifying of the effect upon her of study of the classics and other Chinese literature (note, for example, her translation of the "Precepts of the Lady Pan Chao"), was Florence's attitude toward my Mother, whom, after our marriage, she addressed as Tai-tai. They had been friends since Mother made her first trip to Shanghai in 1922. Mother deeply admired Florence's scholarship, greatly enjoyed her books and lectures, and delighted in her personality. Florence realized fully what Mother had done for, and meant to, me. Her cablegram to Mother in Shanghai, sent from Guernsey the day before our marriage, and Mother's reply, were beautiful and sincere. Had either been selfish in her affection, harmony would have been lacking and a perfect relationship impossible. But it was not so. Both truly welcomed the change in their relations, and each became increasingly devoted to the other. Surely, *very* few men have been as fortunate as I.

To compare the lights radiated by Florence with those of a diamond would be wrong in essence: the brilliance of the diamond is external, hard, and without warmth. To compare them with those of the pearl would be equally erroneous: the pearl, having all colors fused, is without color and connotes softness. If there be in the universe such a phenomenon as accident, certainly Florence's feeling for opals cannot have been accidental. In the opal is a merging of colors without fusion, a glowing of inner lights which is neither hard nor soft, a warm iridescence marked by shades and shadows. The opal has firmness without touch of sentimentality.

Only a poet could have described Florence's eyes, and, then, probably, by the use of clichés—which she loathed. One of the keys to an understanding of her aims and her art as a translator from the Chinese is to be found in her attitude toward clichés. Heartily did she disapprove the method of certain Chinese who,

(11)

to show that they "know English," turn the metaphors of their language into hackneyed Western similes.

Florence's whimsicalities were manifested in a myriad ways. Once I rubbed a finger over, and commented disparagingly on, her "Wheelock nose"; at which she smiled superiorly and observed, "*My* think-so b'long hand*sum*"—a household phrase supplied by one of her mafoos on whose smart appearance she once had commented. He straightened snappily, surveyed himself with satisfaction, and replied, "*My* think-so b'long hand*sum*." Apropos, did she ever tell you of the crushingly laconic comment of her Chinese chauffeur when she found him one day contemplating a bright new motor just out from England, parked next hers, and remarked upon its splendor? "*Can* pass," he replied. Reminiscent of the scandalized retort of her devoted amah when Florence had asked her to make sure that the household staff use care in burning incense before the shrine of the Empress of Heaven in the basement of Wild Goose Happiness House: "What thing! *You* house b'long *my* house. *My* no wantchee *burn* house!" Like all of us old China hands, Florence referred frequently to the innumerable pleasant aspects of relations with Chinese retainers—who are the finest in the world, largely because their ancestors have so long been highly civilized.

My copy of *Firecracker Land,* in which delightful work is found the assertion by the amah of co-proprietorship in Wild Goose Happiness House—which condition later held true of The Grass Hut by the Yellow Reach—bears a double inscription. One reads: "My own copy, Florence Ayscough, 1932"; facing it is the other: "Given to my husband Harley Farnsworth MacNair as *his* own copy (after I had given away the one he owned) on Oct. 27, 1935—by Florence Ayscough MacNair."

Every inscription in a gift copy of her works carried a bit of Florence's personality. Often she signed the Chinese characters of her name: Ai Shih Ke—"Love Poetry Mother," or "Love Poetry Sojourner"—with a quotation carrying an idea of significance to the recipient. My *Fir-Flower Tablets* contains a quotation from Bertrand Russell's *The Problem of China:* "To understand the problem of China we must first know something of Chinese history and culture before the irruption of the White Man"; and: "In memory of many delightful talks, Florence Ayscough,

1922." Later she gave me for it an autograph of Amy Lowell's, cut from one of the letters in the correspondence which was published in January, 1946: *Florence Ayscough and Amy Lowell: Correspondence of a Friendship*.

In April, 1928, she gave me a copy of *Within the Walls of Nanking. By Alice Tisdale Hobart. Proem by Florence Ayscough, D.Litt.*, bearing the statement: "Is Civilization indeed anything but control?"—followed by my name and hers. In October of the same year, Alice Hobart added a quotation from page 151 of the book: "Civilization, perilous possession, is nothing to tamper with." Florence and I had discussed at length, one afternoon in the preceding year, the meaning of civilization and had agreed that its essence is control.

When, in September, 1929, Florence sent me a copy of *Tu Fu: The Autobiography of a Chinese Poet, A.D. 712–770*, she quoted from page 126, preceding my name and hers: "You yourself will be able to grasp the fluttering banners of success—." I choose to consider this an unconscious prophecy of our marriage, six years later to the month, since this was the outstanding success of my life.

One of the two most treasured items in my library is the specially-bound-for-me second volume, in half-leather, dark red, gold lettered, of her translations from Tu Fu, entitled *Travels of a Chinese Poet: Tu Fu, Guest of Rivers and Lakes, A.D. 712–770. By Florence Ayscough. II. A.D. 759–770. Illustrated from Etchings by Lucille Douglass*. This is interleaved with many photographs taken by Gerald Steiner, who accompanied us on a literary pilgrimage by steamer up the Great River through the gorges to Chungking, thence by air to Chengtu—with return to Shanghai by the same means of transportation in reverse.

The most-appreciated photograph inserted is that of Florence, in profile, seated on a high hillside with the Great River and a distant view of Ichang in the background. Smiling, she gazes upward. A close-fitted soft black hat and voluminous cape contrast with the whiteness of her face and the hand resting on her famous alligator handbag. This latter, and its similar-in-style successor, a large black silk bag made by herself, carried, it seemed, almost everything necessary for life's comfort and convenience. Florence used to quote the remark of one who knew her well: "If you need anything, ask Florence; it will be in her attic." *Many* times on that trip and our later journeyings together when *I* wanted something, I "asked Florence"—and she produced it from her handbag! *Always* foresighted and *never* unprepared, before leaving for the Yangtze journey she provided a substitute for her opals in the form of a necklace and earrings of opalescent Peking glass. One of the earrings in this set of what she dubbed her "bandit jewels" is barely visible in the photograph. Under it, after the rebinding of the volume, she wrote: "Ichang, Me—myself—F. A."

On the obverse of the inserted page containing this photograph is Florence's inscription done in purple ink:

Extract from my Note Book [she had divers notebooks of all shapes, sizes, and conditions] Nov 18th 1934
Sunday afternoon opposite Ichang—
 Mr MacNair & Steiner climbed the Pyramid [a high hill]
 I sat on a shoulder of the hill, looking
 down into a valley—Veritable Country
 of the Peach Plossom Fountain—
 people friendly, a fertile place—
 Sounds floated across river from
 Ichang—interesting—could hear:
 people talking, children crying,
 pigs squealing, gongs clanging &
 drums rolling—and above this
 clamor rose the sound of Church
 bells—
 The light was soft & very lovely—

After the volume had been rebound with the added photographs, she wrote:

To Harley Farnsworth MacNair

———

A long time past rain;
 Sorceress Hills dark;
Now, newly bright, all colours
 are embroidered in gold—
 p 235—
In memory of our journey through
Sorceress Gorge—November 1934—
 Florence Ayscough
 Shanghai
 Dec 1—1934

(14)

And in the lower right corner of the page is placed her autograph in Chinese. Not until September 7 of the following year was the full significance of the quotation made manifest to both of us.

In the last of her books to be published while she was here, and which is dedicated to me, she inscribed:

The First Copy—
   For my husband
    with thanks for his advices,
    both the bitter and the sweet—
    Florence Ayscough MacNair
   New York,
   November tenth 1937.

Re mention above of the second volume of *Tu Fu*, I often recall Chesterton's remark, "I thank God I am not so superstitious as to believe in coincidence." Whether one calls it coincidence, fate, or predestination, certainly there seems to have been a Plan for Florence's and my life together—a Plan which, I can now perceive, worked out from the time we met: without hurry, without worry, definitely, step by step, without conscious thought on our part. Certain as I am that we shall again be together (I am writing on the fourth anniversary of her departure), I am almost as sure that we had been together before this incarnation. Time is not of the essence of our relationship. It is incidental and altogether minor in importance.

Who could believe it "accidental" that Florence was born in China and made that country the field of her life-interest? She was pecularly endowed to interpret China to the West in a way in which, in modern times at least, no other Westerner has done. You, who know the attitude of most occidental residents in the treaty ports of China toward the Chinese people and their civilization—also how most Western women spend their days in the Orient—will agree that the most extraordinary aspect of Florence's life was that *she* should have become interested in, and then enthralled by, Chinese studies. Everything in Shanghai, except its location, militated against this: her family duties and her position, the snobbishly compartmentalized social life of international Shanghai, the Chinese general attitude toward

Westerners and that of the majority of Westerners toward the Chinese.

What a pity, apparently, that the greatest, and to the present unbroken, impact of the West upon China should have taken place at a time when the Middle Kingdom was entering, at the end of the eighteenth century, upon another of its periodic declines in power and culture! But perhaps this, too, was in the Great Plan.

To be sure, a few, a very few, representatives of Western governments have interested themselves in the supposedly dying civilization of the East, while a minority of Christian missionaries—including a very few wives—have intelligently, that is, objectively, studied China and its people. But both these groups have tended to approach the subject from particular angles with extremely limited points of view. I remember Florence's mention to me of the shock she received when she was told by a prominent and generally well-informed bishop, long resident in China, that he had never heard of Tu Fu, the greatest of China's poets. The nongovernmental and nonmissionary business groups have, to this day, all but ignored China's cultural importance to the world as well as its intrinsic and innate value.

A student of history, I find life full of the miraculous. There has never been an age more characterized by the miraculous than the one in which we live, and I am not referring mainly to the atomization of life when I say this. By no means the least important example of the miraculous in life, until I *knew* Florence— in contrast to being merely acquainted with her—was the fact that she of all people should have had the desire to do, and then persevered in doing, what she did.

Long before I went to the Orient, from the days of the Boxer Rebellion to the outbreak of the Revolution of 1911–12, China interested me and appealed to my imagination. In my undergraduate days I became aware of the value to China and to the West of Christian missions. But when I applied for a teaching post, it was not for St. John's University in Shanghai but for Boone University in Wuchang. Was it accident that sent me to the former? I doubt it. From the day I landed, on September 24, 1912, I felt *at home* in the country and with the people, precisely as I felt from the time I met Florence: a combination of spiritual and physical comfort, at-oneness—and stimulation.

Florence was a believer in, as she expressed it, "seizing opportunity by the hair." Consider and plan she did, but never did she worry. Even during what I believe she did not realize—until practically the end—was her last illness, she would reply to an occasional query: "When the time comes, we shall know." On being informed one day in St. Andrews that a lumber company was intending to purchase the island (which was framed in the large window of her drawing-room) with the object of removing the timber therefrom, she hurried downtown and bought the island before the company was aware that it had a rival in the market. In Guernsey it was most desirable that 22 Hauteville should have a garage adjoining the main floor of the house. The owner of the tiny plot necessary for the building of a one-car garage asked, what Florence's solicitor considered, an outrageous price—and the solicitor advised postponement of the purchase. Florence hesitated not a moment. The sale was made—and two days later the recent owner became mentally ill. Had Florence not "seized opportunity by the hair," she could not have obtained the land for an indefinite period, if ever.

When the opportunity was offered to me of joining the faculty of the University of Chicago, I did not *wish* to come; I preferred to return to St. John's and China. But when, after having spent a year here, I was at St. Andrews in 1929, and consulted with Florence, she made clear her belief that, for the time at least, my work in China was done and that Chicago offered me an opportunity to do in reverse what I had long been doing in China: help the West to understand the East. Unchanging in my attitude toward China and its people, and acting contrary to my personal preference when I resigned in 1932 from St. John's, I have never regretted following her advice. It was part of the Plan for us.

When she came from Vienna to lecture in the United States in the spring of 1931, and arrived in Chicago, I boarded her train at the Englewood Station, to her great surprise and my great joy, and had a visit before reaching the downtown terminal. That autumn I returned to St. John's for a year. She returned to Vienna and a bit later settled in Guernsey.

When, during the spring of 1934, she returned to Shanghai, it was contrary to her plan; she had intended to go out a year later.

But it became necessary for her to go, and, without hesitation, she went. When I returned to China in the autumn of 1934, less than two years after I had finally resigned from St. John's, this also was contrary to my plan. Had I carried out my intention, we would have missed each other—and the greatest happiness of our lives might not have been attained. Which goes to prove the truth of an old saying in which I profoundly believe: You never know your luck!

In the late summer of 1934 Florence sent me—and I received on September 7, a year to the day before our marriage—the Volume II of *Tu Fu* which was later rebound for me. I saved it to read on the voyage, which I did, carefully and with delight. This volume, as you may remember, bears the subtitle *Tu Fu, Guest of Rivers and Lakes*, and has to do with the poet's sunset years in Szechuen, the building of *his* Grass Hut, and his journey down the Yangtze to greet death on the Poyang Lake. As I read the work—not of one but of two great poets—and studied the etching illustrations by Lucille Douglass, the thought came to me again and again: How delightful it would be if I could persuade Mrs. Ayscough to take a trip *with me* up the Great River to Szechuen! She has been once—but *maybe* she would like to go again.

Having notified her immediately of my sudden change of plan to return a year earlier than I had expected, I had a standing invitation to have tea with her the day after I should land in Shanghai. On reaching St. John's, I found a note of welcome, setting the hour. I went.

She had spent a long, hot summer in the hospital and was pale. We had tea in the drawing-room of The Grass Hut before the moon fireplace, with the large framed rubbing of the fêng-huangs hanging above, and continued our conversation in the First Courtyard. I suggested her need for a holiday and my great desire to visit Tu Fu's temple and garden on the site of the original Grass Hut, autumn with its coolness and color being then at its height. (Two periods of the year above all others remind me of Florence—that moment at height of spring-birth when delicate green leaves outline the otherwise bare branches, and autumn, when colored leaves are falling, and the exquisitely austere beauty of trunks and branches and twigs is again revealed.) Without hesitation she agreed, asking me to make reservations on a through steamer for Chungking.

Because of the more than usual amount of banditry and frequent firings upon steamers on the upper river, incidental to Generalissimo Chiang's anti-Communist campaigns (this was the autumn, you will remember, in which the Great Trek of the Communists via Szechuen, Tibet, and Kansu to Yenan in northern Shensi was begun), I inquired of Captain Taylor of the S.S. "Chi-ping" as to the safety of the proposed journey, picturing "Mrs. Ayscough" as a somewhat timid soul unaccustomed to danger!

In the light of an incident in which both of us had participated more than seven years earlier, this was a peculiarly scandalous misrepresentation on my part, and she and I—to quote one of her phrases—"roared with laughter" when I told her of it and of the Captain's reassurance. I hope Heaven may have pardoned me as quickly as did she.

The event to which I refer had occurred on the afternoon of an early spring day in 1927, when Florence was lecturing in French on Chinese gardens, at the old French Club on Avenue Joffre. In the middle of the address, to which she had invited me, there occurred the sound of a shell passing the building. This was almost immediately followed by the clanging of sections of the fire department on the avenue. A number of the audience hastily withdrew. After a few minutes' pause, Florence serenely inquired—in the language of the occasion—whether it was the wish of those remaining that she continue. Assured that it was, she did so. A few minutes later another really deafening explosion took place which, this time, shook the building—and more of the audience withdrew in even greater haste. Florence remained standing by the reading-desk while those who did not flee dashed to the windows and discussed the situation in most of the languages of Shanghai. When the excitement had become a little less noticeable, Florence, without a tremor in her voice, again, requested the pleasure of the meeting. Several Frenchmen, not to be outdone in gallantry by a woman, or a British subject, assured her of their continued interest—and Florence composedly finished her lecture.

Leaving the hall, we learned that the second detonation had

been caused by a "dud" shell which had struck the wall of the Club about fifty feet from where Florence had been standing. The firing was incident to a sudden change of allegiance on the part of a Chinese warship in the Whangpoo some five miles distant.

To return to the journey of the "After-After-After Three Wanderers"[2]—Florence, Gerald Steiner, and myself—up the Great River: I am sure that if Captain Taylor had taken stock in my representation of the lady as being physically timid, he underwent no illusion as to her moral courage in the course of the voyage. I quote from a letter written en route:

This afternoon, after we had anchored (4:45 p.m.), again "nowhere," about twenty-four miles beyond Wanhsien and while the Captain had come up to talk with us, Mrs. A. caused considerable commotion and "innocent merriment."

On the top deck (where we sit without awning to watch the views) the Steward keeps a number of hens in one small basket. I commented upon the uneasiness of the fowls at various times, and Mrs. A. [a member of the Society for the Prevention of Cruelty to Animals] decided to protest in a friendly, but firm, manner to the Captain against rendering their last days unhappy by such close confinement. She did so, and the Captain replied that he'd had a beautiful wooden cage made for them (which I'd noticed, but supposed it was for wild animals) but that the Steward preferred the basket. Mrs. A. remarked sweetly that this must have disappointed the Captain, to which the Captain equally sweetly replied that he'd *often* been disappointed—for example, he had hoped to reach Chungking this afternoon. Soon, however, he said he would speak to the Steward.

When I came back to the upper deck a few minutes later, I saw that the chickens were in two baskets—and observed to Mrs. A. that, like a Boy Scout, she had done her good deed for the day. Minnie, the cat, and Pete, the poodle (the Captain's own livestock), were now chasing each other around the deck. Suddenly there was a great commotion among the hens, whom the cat every once in a while paused to stalk, and one of the hens climbed out between gaps in the roped top of the basket. While Captain Taylor and the Lieutenant [of the Marines, O'Donnell, who, with a private, a private first class, a corporal, and a sergeant, guarded the "Chi-ping" against possible bandit raids] dove for the hen, another decided to seek healthier regions and more space—and a third followed suit with remarkable agility and promptitude.

Gerald Steiner joined in the chase, while Mrs. A. rushed forward expressing solicitude—but whether for the hens, the Captain, the Lieutenant, Steiner, or Minnie was not quite clear. Then she suddenly re-

[2] See *A Chinese Mirror: Being Reflections of Reality behind Appearance* (London, Boston, and New York, 1925), p. 101.

treated to her chair, overcome with a guilty sense of "misplaced kindness," and remarked to me, an interested onlooker, that she was to blame—and implied that it was as well for her not to be too prominent for the time being.

By this time the Chinese Steward and one or two of his assistants appeared. Between them and the naval and civilian arms of law and order the recalcitrant hens were securely locked in the elegant chicken box [except one that flew overboard and was drowned in the river]—and thus both the Captain and Mrs. A. were happily vindicated. It is hoped that the hens will be comfortable for the remainder of their days.

Although Florence had a decisive mind and was never given to, what she called, "hāvering"—that is, hesitating, shillyshallying, and blowing hot and cold—on an issue, I had been a bit surprised (although I had not expressed it!), and more than a little gratified, at the ease with which I had persuaded her to "grasp opportunity by the hair" in accompanying me up the Great River. The mystery was cleared one afternoon during the return journey from Szechuen as we stood by the ship's rail gazing at the scenery. In the course of the conversation she suddenly queried: "By the way, did you receive my letter addressed to Yokohama?"

"No," I replied. "I received several letters there, but none from you until I reached St. John's and found your note asking me to tea."

"Why, *that* is strange! I wrote telling you of my summer in the hospital and suggesting that we might journey together in the steps of Tu Fu in Szechuen."

When we reached Shanghai, I found the letter, which had been forwarded from Yokohama, containing the suggestion for the trip we had just finished. So—you will further understand why I believe in Plans rather than in Coincidences!

One of the most charming events of the ensuing winter was the dinner to which she invited me at The Grass Hut on the eve of Chinese New Year's to help celebrate the sending on high of the "kitchen god." On a cold, starlit night after dinner, she and her guests, accompanied by the household staff and their relatives and children of numerous degrees of relationship, proceeded to the kitchen to take down the god for the dying year from his place above the stove. We then marched back the length of the house and intervening courts to the front court yard, where the patron saint of the kitchen was placed in a specially-constructed-for-the-occasion paper airplane and burned. Fond of "olo-custom," Florence saw no reason why such should not be modernized, to a degree. She had, of course, consulted the cook *et al.* and obtained their enthusiastic approval to their protector's arriving early in the upper region so that he might render his account while the heavenly bookkeeper was yet fresh and unwearied by the reports of those millions of messengers who would arrive by more conservative means of transportation. Few patron saints of the kitchen have been sent off with more éclat than that of Mme Ai in 1935!

Florence had a sense of the ridiculous equaled only by her dignity. Did she ever tell you the episode of the chewing gum? Immediately prior to sailing for Shanghai after finishing her schooling in Boston, she and her Mother were one day in the neighborhood of a drug store when Mrs. Wheelock remembered that she had recently been told of the efficacy of chewing gum in preventing sea sickness.

"Florence, will you go into this store and ask, please, for a package of Beeman's Pepsin Chewing Gum?"

"*No*, Mother, I will *not*—if *you* want *chewing gum* you must get it *yourself!*"

Accordingly, Mrs. Wheelock, assuming what Florence described as her Mother's most "ice-chesty manner," marched up to a young clerk and requested to know, "Have you Bee-man's Pep-sin Chew-ing Gum?"

"No, madame," replied the clerk, bending forward solicitously but with a glint in his eyes, "we have no Bee-man's Pep-sin Chew-ing Gum—*but* have you *ever* tried *Tutti-frutti?*" Florence dashed from the store to avoid hysterics, while her Mother retreated almost as hastily, but with all sails set, without the specific for *mal de mer*.

I do not remember the occasion of the remark of one who declared, "Florence is so *damned* persistent," but it may well have referred to the time when, at sea and suffering from nausea, she retreated from the dining salon *and returned* either four or five times before triumphantly finishing dinner. She would not give up, and in her later years (see her account, in a letter to Miss

Lowell, of a winter crossing of the Pacific)[3] she completely conquered her tendency toward seasickness.

On our last trip home, while bucking the southwest monsoon in the Indian Ocean, in the summer of 1939, I debated every afternoon for ten days or longer, when the dressing gong was sounded whether to remain comfortably—and safely—on my back or to don dinner jacket and accompany Florence below. She would not deign to advise me, but the force of her example (like that exerted by the emperors of China) and the memory of the Frenchmen who would not be outdone by a woman—and a Britisher at that—always turned me into a Christian Scientist pro tem. I would lurch into my clothes and partake lightly of a full-course dinner—the while noting with satisfaction the withdrawal, midmeal, of men who looked much stronger than I felt. In lieu of Beeman's Pepsin Chewing Gum, I would ruminate and ruminate a piece of bread between courses, while Florence, having composedly advanced from soup to nuts would finally, with the utmost deliberation, peel and seed and consume the last grape on her plate—after which rite we would progress slowly from the salon! It is not by accident that the British have inherited so large a part of the earth. Truly, the dividends of meekness are great.

If not in a Gilbertian sense, Florence was no less sincerely satisfied with her nationality. I used to "point with pride" to the fact that, while I was an American *citizen*, she was but a British *subject*. She remained unimpressed and never considered changing her political status. Indeed, there was every reason why she should not, and the matter was merely one for jesting.

When we reached Shimonoseki from Fusan, early in June, 1939, I, foreseeing another inquisitorial session regarding our passports, decided that we should advance last for inspection. The little Japanese functionary examined and re-examined with care every page of our documents. Then, sucking in his breath: "S-s-s-s"—to me—"this is *your* passport?"

"Yes-s-s."

"S-s-s-s, you are *married?*"

"Yes-s-s."

[3] *Florence Ayscough and Amy Lowell: Correspondence of a Friendship* (Chicago, 1946), pp. 163-64.

"S-s-s-s. This-s-s is-s your *wife's-s* passport?"

"Yes-s-s."

"But-t, *why* your passport is-s 'Merican, and, s-s-s-s, your wife's-s passport, s-s-s-s, is *British?*" Evidently he had not met one before who *could* be an American citizen but would not.

"Ah-h, you s-see, my wife is Brrrittish—and does not *wish* to to be an American!"

Not even the prospect, and the eventuality, of having to leave the United States and re-enter, in order to change her status from that of a visitor to that of a permanent resident, caused her to quail. Bales of red tape had to be unwound; innumerable documents had to be signed and oaths of divers types—and photographs—had to be taken. I all but had a stroke of apoplexy when I received the demands of the Washington bureaucrats (and *we* criticize other governments for their bureaucratic organizations and stiff-necked perversities!) that *I prove* my own citizenship and qualifications to have, to hold, and to maintain an "alien" wife. Through it all, assured that, ultimately, Truth triumphs and Justice prevails, Florence remained as serene as a morning in May.

Finally, we motored to Detroit, crossed the border to Windsor, spent hours in and around the United States consulate, signed more documents, had more photographs taken and waited for their development and acceptance—then crossed back to Detroit. One would have thought I was trying to ooze into the Land of the Free a gory-handed Bolshevist or a fuzzy-headed Hottentot. However, Truth did prevail; Justice (and I) did triumph; the sacrifices to the god of Nationalism proved acceptable; the bales of red tape were neatly rebound—and Florence received a visa for permanent residence in the United States—which had to be renewed only every two years or so and carefully nurtured whenever we traveled abroad!

Some day, the story may—but probably will not—be told of the equally involved but much more joyous and amusing complications with English and Anglo-Norman-French civil and ecclesiastical law which I, chiefly, but Florence also, had to face when she, upon the suggestion of Sir Havilland and Lady de Sausmarez, decided that our marriage should take place in Guernsey instead of in Berlin. I had suggested the latter inasmuch as my friend and colleague, William E. Dodd, was at the time serving as ambassador to Germany, and I believed that he could smooth out the probable difficulties involved in the marriage of two aliens on the Continent.

And, still, why should I not tell *you*, who were so devoted to Florence, the story? The incidents did, after all, constitute part of my tribute to the Incomparable Lady, and so I shall quote again, in part, from letters home.

When I embarked in Quebec . . . . I found two cablegrams. . . . saying Guernsey would be the best place for the marriage as there are no residence requirements—advising that I get a visa and remain on the "Duchess of Richmond" to Southampton (instead of disembarking at Cherbourg) and go thence to Guernsey; also that I must get a "responsible person" to cable a statement [for the Dean of Guernsey: *once* in the history of that island a "foreigner" had contracted a bigamous marriage there!] that I am a bachelor!

On my arrival, Florence told me that, on the Sunday evening before the "Duchess" was to sail on Monday morning from Quebec, she had dined with the De Sausmarezes and had told them of the Berlin marriage plan. After she had returned to 22 Hauteville and retired, the telephone had rung, and the following conversation had taken place with Lady de Sausmarez:

"You know, my dear, Sir Havilland has been thinking over what you said about being married in Berlin, and he believes you are making a mistake." You may remember that Sir Havilland had been chief justice for several years of the British Supreme Court for China, and he was *pretty* well up on law in general.

"Well," replied Florence, rather dazed, "where *shall* we be married then?"

"Why, my dear, here in Guernsey, of course. There will be no difficulty; this is your home! Dr. MacNair can come here instead of meeting you in Cherbourg. You can have the ceremony here and then go to the Continent, according to your plans."

Florence returned to bed, figured out the differences in time between Guernsey and Quebec—and early in the morning hurried to the cable office in St. Peter Port to reach me before I should sail.

Fortunately, I had embarked some four hours before the ship was due to leave. Immediately [after reading Florence's cables and letters],

I went to the officer who supervises passenger traffic. Much talking. Upshot: visa impossible as I was already in the British Empire and such must be obtained *outside* the Empire—obvious, of course. What to do? If I wanted to run the risk of deportation on the next C.P.S.S. leaving Southampton for Quebec, I *might* stay on to Southampton and explain the case to the immigration authorities—otherwise get off at Cherbourg [I had a French visa, of course], obtain a British visa, and cross on another ship to Southampton and thence to Guernsey. All completely simple—like "The Lady or the Tiger." This hardly seemed the sort of trip on which to run risks. Finally, I decided to interview the Captain. He was very pleasant—and assured me there was nothing *he* could do; he "runs" the "Duchess," *not* the immigration bureau. Again, simple and obvious. As there was *nothing to do*—except choose one of the horns of the dilemma—I cabled to Guernsey: "Visa impossible. Disembark Cherbourg. Cross Southampton. Guernsey. Hurrah."

I got a letter off to Vice-President Woodward—as a "responsible person"—telling him of my plans (confidentially) and asking him to cable "ofishially" to Flonsaisco declaring me to be a bachelor! Then I sat back at ease, believing it would take no more than a day or two extra in any case.

But I hadn't taken into account that I was engaged to no "ordinary" woman without brains—or influence. The next day I was in the smoking lounge, writing, when a steward appeared with a marconigram and asked me to sign on the dotted line. I did. Then I read the message—and grinned fore and aft. This was the message: "Proceed Southampton. Governor has directed immigration officer allow you come direct Guernsey ignoring lack of visa."

And thus, even in marriage, I continue gaily through life breaking rules and regulations which, however good and necessary, under ordinary conditions, *should* at times be broken. It isn't everyone, however, who can "break into" England without a visa!.... It's really lots of fun to get rules broken. On the other hand, of course, it's fortunate that one can't *always* get them broken: if I had succeeded last year in getting the nine-quarter residence rule at the U. of C. broken, I'd not be on my way to Guernsey this year to break rules and marry Florence Ayscough! Isn't life amusing? And doesn't it look, as one considers the various factors, that Heaven *wills* I should marry the Lady?

So, after catching my breath—and obliterating the grin, I sent another wireless: "Flonsaisco, Guernsey. Enthusiasm rampant. Thank Governor Benten [i.e., Governor *and* Benten Sama]. Nothing like marrying Lady of Guernsey." And I'll wager Florence had a good laugh when she got that wireless with her breakfast tray.....

The allusion to Benten Sama has to do with another of Florence's delightful good-luck "superstitions." Many years ago there came into her possession a most exquisite little figure in Japanese ivory of Benten Sama seated on a deer—with detachable horns. Of her, Will. H. Edmunds in his *Pointers and Clues to the Subjects of Chinese and Japanese Art* (London, [1934]) writes, in part:

. . . . "The Goddess of Eloquence and Learning"; or "She who governs the treasures"; but usually associated with the *Shichi Fuku Jin* or Seven Gods of Felicity as the Goddess of Music, the ideal of feminine beauty, and the only female member of the group [analogous to Florence's being the only woman to be elected to *Honorary* Membership in the North China Branch of the Royal Asiatic Society?!]. . . . .

Her worship in Japan is principally as the Goddess of Love, and as the Giver of Wealth. Her shrines are usually set upon islands, as at Enoshima. . . . .

When Florence and Gerald Steiner and I were traveling in Japan during the spring of 1935, we made a pilgrimage to the summit of Hiei-zan, the protecting mountain above Kyoto. There we happened upon a roadside booth offering for sale the Japanese signs of the zodiac with explanations of the animals under whose influence, according to their birthdays, individuals are born. Florence found that her patron animal was the Rat; mine was the Dragon! From this discovery came one of her nicknames for me: "Son of the Dragon." The other—that of "The Good Companion"—had eventuated from our journey of the preceding autumn up the Great River.

Florence was not certain that she relished being under the patronage of the Rat, but I reminded her of the delightful character in Kenneth Grahame's *The Wind in the Willows*, a copy of which I mailed to her as she sailed for England some two months later. This, and the telegraphing of red roses, which reached her as she sailed from Montreal, consoled her, to a degree, for the trick played on her by the Nipponese god of fortune. To make the record complete, although I think you need no reassurance, I will add that I *never* addressed Florence as "Daughter of the Rat"!

As she always wore her opals, even when in mourning, feeling, as she once remarked to me, "not fully dressed without them," so also she never traveled without the figure of Benten Sama securely fitted in its blue cloth-covered box with snap-on cover—in her alligator bag. Benten Sama accompanied her to the hospital at the last. "Offerings" were often made to Benten by

Florence, and by her friends, and were placed in the little box at the feet of the goddess. Among such were several grains of burnt rice dug up in May, 1939, on the site of a granary in the ancient kingdom of Paikche in southwestern Korea. The granary and its contents were destroyed during the first war between China and Japan in the seventh century of our era. A tiny cowrie and one or two very old and small coins were also among the offerings to Benten Sama.

On numerous occasions I watched Florence greet Benten vocally and by touching lightly the delicate face of the figure. If at sea the elements were not auspicious, she would smile at Benten and in dulcet tones request good weather—for my sake more than her own. She would then turn to me and say, "Now, *you* greet Benten, also, and ask her for smooth seas!" And I would, with alacrity—for Florence and Benten Sama were one to me—and I would equally complaisantly join her in bowing nine times to the new moon, the while registering gratitude to Heaven that that luminary appears not at midday!

Florence's whimsical humor and lightheartedness were never-failing sources of joy. Shortly before one holiday season, in reply to my request for suggestions, she addressed an envelope: "To His Excellency Father Christmas % H. F. MacNair, Esq.,"containing the following:

DEAR SAINT NICK:

I know that you like to know the desires of those whom you propose to visit, therefore I now—herewith—express my own—
Item one—Food for the Mind—
    A book by Derk Bodde—as per enclosed notice—
Item two—
    Chinese Themes in American Verse, by W. R. North
Item three—roasting pan as per enclosed note—
Item four—Dutch Oven as pictured—

Yours sincerely and respectfully
FLORENCE AYSCOUGH MACNAIR

With the exception of a calligraphic roll of the year 1103 by Mi Fu (or Fei), entitled *Mi Yüan-Chang shu Hsü Hun shih chuan* ("Mi Yüan-Chang Writes Poems by Hsü Hun—A Hand-Scroll"),[4] the only gift, *relatively worthy* of Florence, which I was ever able to

---

4 See *Monumenta Serica* (Peking), Vol. IV (1939), Fasc. 2.

get for her was a pair of jewel trees of the Ch'ien Lung period which are reputed to have been presented by the emperor to a high official. With jade leaves and flowers of semiprecious stones and seed-pearls, they stand in ornate silver containers, typical of eighteenth-century Chinese art. They were said to have been held by the descendants of the recipient in the family home outside Peking. Fearful of loss at the hands of Japanese—or, possibly, other—soldiery or bandits, their owner smuggled them into the city, early in 1939, in a load of cabbages. In the brilliant sunlight of northern China they shone magnificently, and Florence, who for years had wanted a pair of such ornaments and had never been able to find them, at once announced that she would be delighted to have them. Unfortunately, the light of the sun as it illumines Chicago is not like that of Peking, and not until my brother-in-law, Gerald Steiner, hit upon the idea of mounting not directly visible neon lights behind and below them could their beauty be appreciated here. This he did as a Christmas gift to Florence in 1941. Being in the hospital, she never saw them in their restored beauty, although she appreciated an excellent photograph which Gerald made for her.

Before and after our marriage, to mark some more than ordinarily happy experience, Florence used to write for me, on her fir-flower paper, a little essay—somewhat reminiscent of a *fu*, except, of course, that it was not rhymed—which she would call "A Present." None of these "Presents" has been published, but they contain some of her most charming thoughts and expression thereof.

If Yang Kuei-fei was as fascinating as Florence (but I am sure she was not, since *she* was not a scholar and *her* character was marked by lightmindedness, extravagance, and vindictiveness), I can well understand how the Bright—but not *too* Bright—Emperor could dispense with a throne for her. However, while Florence enjoyed as *drama and romance* the *story* of the Lady Yang and her imperial lover, and made a beautiful translation of Po chü-i's "Ballad of Endless Woe" (which I hope to publish along with her other last translations, including a group of hymns used in the ritual of the sacrifices at the Altar of Heaven), she would not have been a friend of the leading characters in that tragedy had she lived in the days of the T'ang Dynasty.

Do you ask how I know? The answer is simple and the proof sufficient: Florence was inexpressibly shocked and coldly indignant when Edward VIII abdicated. She had told me, years before, in the course of one of our tea conversations before the moon fireplace in The Grass Hut, that it was commonly doubted in England whether the Prince of Wales would ever accept the kingship. But, when the time came, and he mounted the throne, only to treat his position lightly and shortly abdicate, she felt that he had "let down the Empire" and that he had no right to place his personal happiness ahead of the welfare of his peoples. To my suggestion that, after all, Edward had devoted twenty-five or more years of his life to serving as a salesman of empire and that, possibly, he deserved a respite and the pleasure of leading a life of his own, she turned a deaf ear. That was the one subject which we thereafter avoided. When others discussed the problem, I smiled—but Florence turned to stone.

It was an interesting commentary on her profound sense of duty and the fitness of things. She, the Unitarian student of literature and art, had a stronger sense of obligation and morality than had I, the Episcopalian student of history. Life is full of ironies; indeed, the irony of history is to me one of that subject's most absorbing components.

In contrast to Florence's austerity in regard to what some call "the eternal verities," she could leap with agility from the serious to the, if not ridiculous, at least lighter side of life. For example, as a result of her researches into certain phases of the archeology of Guernsey, she made discoveries with respect to the primitive art of Le Déhus; the statue menhir, called La Gran'Mère du Chimquière at St. Martin's Church; and the statue menhir in the Castel Church yard on that island; and, with the aid of Gerald Steiner, her secretary, photographed them. In consequence, she was invited to present a paper, illustrated by colored slides, before the International Congress of Prehistoric and Protohistoric Sciences held in London, in August, 1932.[5]

[5] According to the London correspondent of the *Guernsey Evening Press*, August 15, 1932: "The Congress passed a special vote of thanks to Dr. Ayscough for the privilege of seeing her photographs of the Guernsey antiquities. Several of the scientists remarked that these were by far the best archaeological photographs they had ever seen. Besides showing details so far unrecorded, the pictures cleared up a number of misconceptions based on comparatively hasty observation. In fact, there is no published description of the carvings but

Florence attended all the sessions for two days. On the morning of the third day she debated with herself as to her ability to stand another meeting. Her sense of duty prevailed—until she reached the entrance of the rather drab hall. She paused at the door, looked over the assembly once more—and, then, as she reported to me some four years later, with a laugh: "I turned around and went as fast as I could to the most expensive hat shop in London, and bought myself a hat!"

Another example of her whimsical humor occurs to me in connection with our marriage. In the spring of 1935, before returning from Shanghai to Guernsey, she had several dresses made. The details tried her patience, especially that of standing to be fitted. To her friend, Marian Liddell, she sighed, "I might *just as well* be having a trousseau made."

To which came the reply: "Well, perhaps a bridegroom *might* be found."

"*Never*," was the instant retort. But on our wedding day she cabled Mrs. Liddell, then in Chicago: "Bridegroom found. Married Dr. MacNair today."

To return, after these somewhat lengthy digressions, to the international complications of our marriage:

Wednesday, Sept. 4. . . . . We are due in Southampton *ca.* 4:00 P.M. From one of the stewardesses, whose home is in Guernsey, I learned last

---

has erred on some point—it has been been said, for example, that La Gran'mère has neither arms nor girdle, both of which were shown clearly in the photographs, although they are not easily seen by ordinary inspection. Another moot point shown in the photographs are the circles, or disks or bosses, in the diadem on both the goddess figures. Do these represent hair, or are they, as Dr. Ayscough suggests, a faint reminiscence of the circlet of snakes to be found on similar statues in Asia Minor and the Mediterranean? . . . .

"At the end of the lecture the enthusiastic audience asked for several of the slides to be repeated in order to show points on which there was interested discussion. . . . ."

On the following day the *Guernsey Evening Press* carried another article, with additional illustrations and with the following statements *inter alia:* "Our London Correspondent states that the great triumph of Dr. Asycough's lecture was the photographic records (a feat hitherto believed impossible) of the strange carvings on the underside of the great capstone of Le Déhus. A fascinating point of difference between this and the other carved stones of Guernsey is that where the other two famous statues seem to show primitive man's attempt to honour the great 'Mother Principle' in the universe, the face in Déhus is apparently that of a bearded man, looking watchfully toward the entrance; set there perhaps to guard the tomb. On the lower part of the figure are many hitherto unnoticed scribings, fraught with unknown significance.

"The face appears at the head of this capstone. The remarkable photograph reproduced above was obtained by Dr. Ayscough after persistent effort under great difficulty in a most inaccessible position. . . . ."

night that I can get a night boat from Southampton to Guernsey—and I hope the crossing won't be like ours [Mother's and mine] from St. Malo to Guernsey in 1932! This will put me in there about 7:00 A.M. . . . .

On Monday afternoon, I received another marconigram from Guernsey saying that I shall be met in Southampton by the U.S. Consul —this, I suppose, to aid me with the immigration authorities. Between the Consul and the Governor of Guernsey I ought to be able to land— *somewhere*. . . . .

. . . . Some of the time I feel as if I were in a dream and that it can't be possible that I am to have *such* a wife. In all the world I could not find another whose charm would appeal to me as greatly, or one whose interests so completely dovetail with, and complete, my own. She is able to help me so much; I *hope I* can aid her. . . . .

. . . . It's a lovely, lovely day: the deep blue sea is flecked with whitecaps; the gulls are flying around by the score; the ship is steady; the sun is shining brightly; my bags are ready for landing; and—I am happy.

Despite my marconigram armaments, I felt self-conscious without a visa and at facing an inquisition, so I placed myself at the end of the line. In the meantime, I became aware of interested glances in my direction by two men standing near the passport inspector. I informed the latter that arrangements had been made for me to land in England en route to Guernsey without a visa. He appeared not visibly impressed and proceeded to put me through a catechism which made me glad I had had foresight to seek the last position in the line! Finally, he demanded to know *why* I was going to Guernsey. I smiled and replied, "Well, if you *must* know, I am going there to be married." Thereupon *he* smiled— tactfully forbearing from asking me if I was a bachelor—and admitted: "Yes, I *knew* that all the time!" Thereupon the two who had been eyeing me, discreetly, advanced and announced that they were both from the United States consulate: one was Mr. F. Willard Calder, representative of Mr. Consul Travers; the other, Mr. Pack, had been sent to see my baggage through the customs—without inspection—and then to help me get my ticket for Guernsey. Never had I been received with such éclat; never do I expect to be so received again.

My mail in Southampton contained letters from Florence— and Benten Sama—also a charming photograph of Benten, on her deer, bearing a heartening (if I had needed it) message of welcome to Guernsey. Benten Sama had provided the most perfect of Atlantic, and English Channel, crossings, and I shall not cease to be grateful to her!

Not until my landing in St. Peter Port did I learn at what time the ceremony was to take place. As soon as I had breakfasted at 22 Hauteville, Florence said, "*Now*, you must go to the Police Office to register and tell them how long you plan to stay in Guernsey; all *aliens* have to do this immediately after landing." I think she rather enjoyed my being an alien for a change; *she* had had to be grouped with that ilk on the "Empress of Japan" before we disembarked at Victoria, prior to going down the Sound to Seattle on the preceding June 4. "But," she added, "*I* will go with you."

Whenever possible, and she very often made it possible, she walked with, or drove, me to my office at the University during the time she was here, and not rarely she would walk a good part of the way, or come with the car, to meet me on my return. How often I still see her advancing toward me on Wood-lawn Avenue in the becoming red dress she so frequently wore!

After my registering with the police, she said, "And now we must go to the Office of the Government Secretary for you to thank the Governor for his aid, and then to the office of the Dean of Guernsey, so that you may obtain the license." When we had obtained this crucial document, she continued: "Now, we must call on the vicar of the church in the parish in which my home is located and obtain his waiver to performing the ceremony. You will pay him his fee for *not* performing the ceremony, and explain who *is* to perform it, and why!"

This was in accord with the law of the island, going back to the days of William of Normandy or earlier, which decrees that a marriage shall take place within the parish church of the bride and shall be performed by the rector—minimum fee ten shillings! With his consent, after receiving his fee, the marriage service may be held in another parish church.

Florence felt that I would prefer to have the ceremony in the Church of Ste Marie du Castro—commonly referred to as the Castel Church—in which Sir Havilland and Lady de Sausmarez had been married, a much more historic and interesting (thir-teenth-century, double-naved small Gothic) structure than the one in the parish of which 22 Hauteville happens to be located.

So—we called on the vicar who had been ensconsced in *her* parish church since she had left Guernsey and whom she had never seen, and I explained and requested his waiver and paid him the fee for not marrying us!

"Now," said Florence, "we must call on the rector of the Castel Church and make arrangements for the ceremony *there*." And we did, and had a most delightful call, and discovered that he had served for several years in the diocese of Pittsburgh, Pennsylvania, under Bishop Whitehead, who had confirmed me when I was about thirteen years of age. We also found that the Reverend Peter Mezny was a relative of the Mezny in Shanghai, of many years ago, of *Mezny's Miscellany*. (Do you remember that periodical?) And so, the minister and I felt fairly well acquainted before we met at the altar two days later!

Perhaps, even in a privately printed work for our good friends only, I should not go further on this subject. But I believe I shall not be misunderstood, and I shall, accordingly, quote once more from my letters to Mother and Hazel:

SAUSMAREZ MANOR, ST. MARTINS, GUERNSEY
Our Wedding Day, September 7, 1935

It is almost twelve noon—and the ceremony is to be at twelve-thirty. *But* I must start a letter to my Beloved Mother and sister before leaving for the church.

It is a *gorgeous*, a truly magnificent, day, sunny and mild. I am supremely happy. The *only* imperfection (and Heaven does not *permit* perfection) is the lack of you two dear ones to witness the ceremony. I *know* you are with me in spirit—you will have figured out the exact difference in time between Shanghai and Guernsey, and, while we stand at the altar, I shall feel your presences. . . . . Major P. D. Carey, a friend of Florence's, is acting as best man—but *I* am *really* the Best Man, for I am the one who is marrying the one woman in the world—for *me*.

I am writing at the desk in the guest room of the Manor, which, in part, dates back to 1350. The room was used by Sir Havilland's grandparents. It overlooks the most lovely of formal English gardens—lawns, trees, shrubs, and flowers. Lovely.—Must close now and go down to the car. . . . .

FÜRSTENHOF HOTEL, BERLIN
September 15, 1935

To go on where I left off: some five minutes after I stopped, Lady de S. came to my room to say that the car was waiting and that it was time

(34)

to start to the church. She and I drove together, I seeing her to the door of the nave where the ceremony was to take place, while I went through the other nave to the sacristy to wait with Major Carey and the priest until Florence should arrive with Sir Havilland. A couple of minutes before they came Major Carey and I *processed* to the chancel steps, where we waited until Florence's car appeared. I looked down the nave, grinning cheerfully at Florence as she came up on Sir Havilland's arm. But would *she* look at *me*? Not much—she didn't even *glance* at me when she took her place by my side—and there was nothing I could do about it, for I feared that if I stepped on her toes she might say "Ouch" and create a scene. She approached the steps to the measures of the Lohengrin march.

Mr. Mezny, the rector, was waiting for us. He used the service of the revised American Prayer Book, which has the double advantage over the English service (which I amused myself in reading the next day in Jersey at evening prayer) of leaving out the physiological references to the worth-whileness of marriage *and* of being short and snappy.

When I placed the ring on her finger, I lifted her hand and kissed it (not loudly, but well!), which took her completely by surprise but did not displease her—and (I was told later) pleased some of the ladies in the congregation who had not before seen the sacrifice of an English bride to an American barbarian. They felt the affair to be less painful, I suppose.

The ceremony took about ten minutes. My throat got a little lumpy once or twice, but my voice was clear and determined. (I always *do* come through in a crisis, you know.) Florence's voice was low but clear—and she, too, showed no hesitation. My mind was a medley during the affair—but very clear. I felt no excitement and was at no time in danger of fainting! I thought of you both, and of Donald and Frances, a good part of the time, and felt you were with me. Like the woman, who told her children "always to remember that their Mother was a McGraw," I knew you'd want me to do my best—and, if I do say it as hadn't orter, my best that day was *quite* good! I was at ease in my mind, for I was marrying the one woman whom I'd loved for years, though not until this summer had I hoped—with expectation—to marry her.

Florence was *lovely* in an extremely smart black lace dress over white satin with the sauciest black velvet hat, a sort of liberty-cap, you ever could imagine. Her bouquet (I tried to get orchids) was a sheaf of pink lilies and asparagus fern with sprigs of myrtle cut from a tree at the Manor by the De Sausmarez gardener. Major Carey and I wore sprigs of it in our buttonholes. . . . .

The wedding ring I purchased in St. Peter Port—with Florence as judge! You'd have smiled if you could have seen the nonchalant and un-blushing manner in which I walked into that shop and demanded to see such. You might have thought that I was a movie actor marrying for the 'steenth time. The band is of platinum, narrow, in ten sections: five plain and five set with tiny diamonds. It is *extremely* simple, but distinctly "stylish," and glints beautifully with the movement of her hand. As an engagement ring, I gave her my ring set with that very ancient "ant-nose" Chinese coin which Mr. H. C. Lieu-ti-chih gave me in Shanghai years ago. She likes it very much—in fact, she asked me for it, which delighted me. About thirty to thirty-five witnessed the ceremony. The church was decorated with lillies.

After the ceremony, Florence took my left arm and we, plus the clergyman, the best man, and Sir Havilland and Lady de Sausmarez, proceeded to the sacristy to sign the marriage register—the De S's and Major Carey serving as witnesses. Then we left the church "to the strains of the Mendelssohn wedding march"—which I had certainly never expected to hear played for *me* and *my* wife!

Gerald snapped pictures of us [one of which showed Florence, as we left the building, looking across to the goddess statue menhir standing amidst the trees of the Castel Church yard] which you will see in due course. We then drove back to the Manor. Assembled there twelve of us: we two; the De S.'s; Lady de Sausmarez' sister, Mrs. Mulloy; Mr. and Mrs. Mezny; Major and Mrs. Carey; Colonel and Mrs. de Putron; and Mrs. Symons. Our health was drunk, and we went to lunch. Very nice and jolly and dignified—no chaffing. Then we drove to Florence's home for her to change to her going-away dress—mauve silk with raisin-colored hat and cloak—positively *chick!!* She looked perfectly lovely. Gerald took us down to the boat for Jersey late in the afternoon.

As said before, the day was absolutely perfect—and so was the crossing, about one and one-half hours. . . . . We stayed in St. Hélier until Tuesday afternoon. Gerald brought the car over that morning and transshipped it to the afternoon boat for St. Malo. Again we had a perfect crossing and a perfect time.

It is *now* after ten P.M., and we are dining in our room. We are both hungry, so—having landed ourselves on the Continent—I'll pause, like Sinbad the Sailor, until next time to describe something of our trip from St. Malo to Berlin. That has been perfect, too—and we are blissfully happy.

[Later:] The *murasaki* (i.e., violet) dress with flame gauze sleeves is the one Florence wore at the dinner we gave for her in Chicago in 1931. It was made in Vienna by a genius. She remembered how much I had liked it and brought it to wear at our first dinner after marriage. It is very lovely. [Later:] Florence insists, in tones of anguish, that I add that the dress has been remade for this occasion! Anyhow, it's lovely. . . . .

The moonlight in St. Malo was marvelous. We did not go to Mont St. Michel, as we had planned, because the stupid ones in Jersey failed to make arrangements for taking off the Tan Jaguar from the S.S. "St.

Patrick" the night we arrived. We therefore spent the night in St. Malo and set off the next morning across Brittany and Normandy. . . . .

The Duchess Uta and the Duchess Regilindes are two lovely stone figures in the Cathedral at Naumburg. Florence particularly wanted me to see them, which we did—after waiting for a wedding to be held, while we had tea in a shop near by. . . . .

Despite the *very* rough crossing from Ostend to Dover, Florence and I were not sick—I should say, *I* was not sick: Florence never is seasick. I have always sworn I'd *never* go to Europe on a wedding trip and run the dangers of *mal de mer*. I had to go to Europe *for* a wedding trip—not *on*. But it goes to show one had best not swear!

The ring ordered in London is *the* engagement ring. It was impossible for Florence to wear with the wedding ring *my* ring, with its heavy mounting. Therefore, I ordered one designed by Florence. It reached us as we embarked at Greenock; it is beautiful *and* unique *and* carries the Chinese motif. The platinum band matches that of the wedding ring. Three rows of small diamonds "parallel" the two longer sides of the dark-green bronze coin with its rubbed old face showing eyes and mouth, while three larger ones are at the base. The mounted coin reaches out at one side to the knuckle. The ring fits perfectly with the wedding ring, and the combination is very beautiful and out of the common—like the wearer. . . . .

Did I tell you, by the way, that *my* wedding ring is a platinum-covered old gold ring set with a lovely Ceylon cats-eye? It had belonged to Florence's mother and is extremely pretty. She gave it to me on The Day. . . . . The bugle has sounded for our last dinner on the "Duchess of Richmond"—at least for this trip. I must dress. We disembark about 7:00 A.M. tomorrow. . . . .

The mention above of the Tan Jaguar reminds me of another of Florence's charmingly imaginative propensities—that of bestowing personality upon, with consequent affection for, inanimate objects in daily use. Incidentally, in the predecessors of the Tan Jaguar and his successor, the Cloud Dragon, was suspended a centuries-old small Chinese bronze mirror (symbolic of "Reflections of the Reality behind Appearance"), secured by a piece of orange-colored cloth; also there was present a small figure of St. Christopher, patron saint of travelers.

Very convenient, too, was her giving of a name to several rooms in the House of the Wu-t'ung Trees. Our bedroom is "The Silver Box," in which is suspended from the central light the carved figure of a dove, symbol of the Holy Spirit, which Florence purchased in Stockholm on a lecture journey; my dressing

(37)

room, "The Ming Bedroom," was named for a canopied structure dating to the Ming era; Mother's room was, of course,
known as "Tai-tai's Room." Not long before she went away,
Florence wistfully asked one night in the hospital, just before
falling asleep: "*Will* you take me back to 'The Silver Box'?"

The pieces of luggage which went with us in the car were all
named. There were, for example, Lulu and Leila, small dressing
cases, and Necessaire, which held her toilet articles, and Fürstenhof, which held mine. Thus at the end of a day's motoring, the
pieces wanted overnight in the hotel could be identified without
description. And, always, there was Tea-Basket, containing
inter alia a small, heavily oxidized-with-age Japanese teapot
which, on pain of death, was never to be polished—reminiscent
of Florence's refusal to have the earth of grave burials removed
from *her* bronzes or potteries. When I would carefully, with
brush and water, clean *my* purchases and offer to "improve the
looks" of hers, she would reply, "No, thank you. I paid for the
dirt—and I will keep it!"

With Tea-Basket handy, we could pause by the side of a country road and quickly prepare a tea or even a meal, enjoy a fine
view, and rest on blankets a while before continuing the drive.
Tea-Basket was most comforting during the early September
days of 1939—after the outbreak of war in Europe—in Room
403 of the Ivanhoe Hotel in Bloomsbury. From our windows we
could observe phases of the evacuation of the British Museum.

Referring to tea with Florence—again, and so often—I think
of the early mornings at home on which we would have it in bed
before breakfast, while I would read aloud to her, or she to me,
and we would discuss her latest translation of a Chinese poem
or essay.

And this, in turn, brings to mind our evenings together in the
library by a wood fire when I would read to her while she would
restring her necklace—once a month or so—or paint slides or
work at restoring an unusually large and terribly tattered old
piece of pomegranite-red and gold *k'eh-ssu* tapestry which had
belonged to her Mother. She never completed the restoration,
but the Art Institute was happy to receive it as part of the collection given and named in memory of her.

What a *grand* time we had together in the library! Especially was this so after we had enlarged it to hold her huge Ming Dynasty gold-and-silver- and black-laquered Buddhist monastery cabinets (which were sent from Shanghai in *one* box—and delivered to the house by *one* man and) which were placed one on each side of the window overlooking the terrace and the garden.

Second only in beauty to these cabinets is the twelve-paneled carved *huang-hua-li* wooden screen of the Ch'ien Lung reign with its original monochrome paintings of orchids. These panels were drawn to Florence's attention one day when we were on Furniture Street, down in the Chinese City of Peking. They were in a dark corner and covered with dust. We asked the proprietor to have them taken out to the street for inspection. They reached to the eaves of the building. She studied them a while, then, shaking her head slowly, said, "There really isn't *any* place in which we could use them, is there?"

"Yes," I replied, "I think they will solve the problem of covering the bookcases in the lower part of the library"—a problem which had puzzled us and the architect a bit when the plans were being drawn. We did not want open shelves in the addition to the room, as there are in the original part, lest it be given an institutional appearance. We went back to Mrs. Calhoun's, got out the architect's blueprints, and, delving into her handbag, Florence drew forth a steel tape measure ("Ask Florence—it will be in her attic")—and, of course, found that the panels *exactly* fitted the space. As usual, Heaven was on our side.

In the library, across the window looking over the terrace and garden, we placed the long narrow *huang-hua-li* table which I had gotten in Soochow many years before, and whose carvings harmonize perfectly with those of the Ch'ien Lung screen. On this we placed the T'ang pottery horse, named by Florence after T'ang T'ai-tsung's famous charger, Shine White in the Night, which we had obtained in Peking, Then Gerald photographed the unit on a snowy day—and that is the origin of the Christmas card which you and others of our friends received in 1939.

On a smaller table, on the upper level of the room, Florence placed her Yunnan marble screen with its gray-white-black design created-by-nature which can be interpreted as a water spout at sea or a great tree on a hillside.

In the library, too, were placed on the lower level of the room, the silk and gold-thread nine-clawed imperial dragon rugs with the characters, woven at one end of each, naming the pavilions of the palace within the Forbidden City for which they were designed. On the upper level was placed the blue-and-gold wool rug of the Ch'ien Lung period. The palace rugs were Mother's and mine (Mother would never allow hers to be put on the floor, so it was thrown over a chesterfield), while the long, narrow Ch'ien Lung rug, and the *sang de boeuf* porcelain vase on a high square Chinese stand in another window, had belonged to Florence's Parents. All these will, I hope, eventually be added to the Art Institute Collection previously mentioned.

After spending the first delightful evening with our friends, Herbert and Alice Hastings Bradley, African big-game hunters, in their magnificent trophy room, another proof of Heaven's will occurred to me. "*Suppose*," said I to Florence, on returning home, "that *I* had been a big-game hunter in Africa, how would we *ever* have merged our collections?"

In the library, Florence read to me, chapter by chapter as she wrote them, and we discussed critically, *Chinese Women Yesterday and Today*. In turn, I read to her piecemeal *The Real Conflict between China and Japan*, several translations for which she had made. The more we read aloud to each other, and criticized and discussed our writings, the more we became convinced of the great value of the process. Among her papers I found a note in her handwriting: "The Chinese feel that the only way to appreciate literature is by reading—reading aloud—reading more and more until the sounds and rhythm become part of one." Every writer should, before publishing, read aloud to a competent and friendly critic the product of his mind and pen. But, now, with Florence and Mother both gone, I have no one to read to.

When we read for pleasure only, I generally did it, especially in the evening, since Florence's voice was so soothing that I would fall asleep when she read—even if we were at the denouement of a mystery story: *My* voice, happily, did *not* have that effect on her!—Now (May 5), I must stop writing and go to church. I go often to the Unitarian Church to sit where she and I used to sit. There she seems to be especially with me, and I always hope that the adjoining chair will not be occupied. On the altar last Sunday again I had flowers placed in memory of her departure.

Despite our long friendship and our years together, it was not until I went through her files that I realized fully—if even then—the breadth and variety of Florence's interests in many cultures. In Chinese, French, and German, as well as in English, there were materials relating to Buddhism, Taoism, Lamaism (she had met the Panchen Lama and witnessed a Kalashakra ceremony in Hangchow which had resulted in study for the writing of a paper for the 1938 Brussels Congress of Orientalists), painting, poetry, folk songs, the theater, marriage rites, and other aspects of the life of China and other lands.

These interests were further evidenced in the several hundreds of colored slides which were presented this spring to the China Institute, Inc. (New York), in her memory and that of Lucille Douglass, who helped her, and whom she helped, so greatly. In her illustrated lectures Florence was most meticulous in her acknowledgment of Miss Douglass' aid with the slides. Also, she insisted on dividing with her the royalties from the books which Miss Douglass illustrated.

A large envelope contained clippings, on early man, on tea, on some five-hundred-year-old seeds of lotus found in Manchuria; a typed quotation from "There Shall Be No Night" (which stated one of Florence's credos); an article on Hus, a "pioneer of liberty"; a Phi Beta Kappa address by Robert Maynard Hutchins on "The Aim of Education"; a notice of George Lansbury's *This Way to Peace;* a condensation of Dr. Gustave Ekstrom's *Your Psychic Self;* and an article on George Aden Ahgupuk, an Alaskan Eskimo artist. Truly can it be said that nothing relating to humanity was alien to Florence—and nowhere was this more clearly or more often demonstrated than in her relations with the Chinese of many types with whom she came in touch: her household staff; her teachers; the "North-of-the-River" refugees, some of whom for a season became her neighbors, as did the members of a Buddhist monastery (built on the site of the garden after Wild Goose Happiness House was sold), in whose services she became greatly interested; and the modern-minded intelligentsia of Shanghai. I am sure that her friends Tu Fu and Amah must have been among the first to welcome Florence to the Western Paradise.

You, who heard Florence's lectures before the Royal Asiatic Society and elsewhere in Shanghai, will agree with me that they were masterpieces—the products of a great artist who put herself into them as any artist puts his best into whatever channel he uses for the expression of his genius. In her lectures there was nothing haphazard. Nothing was left to chance or to momentary inspiration—except, occasionally, the choice of a word. The illustrations and the text were fused into a perfect whole, which was the result of deep study by a mind attuned to the good, wherever found. Convinced of the basic rectitude of man, Florence found evidences of it everywhere—but she was convinced that "in order to stand, the Superior Man must learn," and the story of Mencius' mother and the cutting of the web strongly appealed to her.

In her notes on the great patriot Yo Fei, Florence noted in parenthesis: "The Chinese have a saying that at three one can settle what a child will be at eighty." One who studies her photographs from babyhood through the years will agree with this: the inquiring meditativeness of the eyes, the poise, the strength, the serenity—all these are to be observed in her girlhood photographs. To these are added humor, a sense of having accomplished the work which she was intended to accomplish— and *joy* in those of the last years.

In the same notes Florence quotes the declaration of Yo Fei's father: "Having a son like this, I have no grief in life." This I may paraphrase: Having had Florence for wife, I have no grief save in losing her physical presence—and no wish save to be reunited with her.

In concluding my tribute, again I hesitate. Is it well to include part of a letter written to a dear friend of ours shortly after Florence went away? I believe it is, since I am writing for friends who will, I am sure, understand. None but a friend will take the time to read this, but if he does—what matter? I quote:

May 3, 1942

DEAR MISS [ADELA] BARRETT:

I have just been going through Florence's things packed by her nurse at the hospital the morning she was released from suffering. It opens the

WHEN WE WERE VERY YOUNG   SERIOUSLY CONTEMPLATING A
                                          PARTY

wounds all over—so I'll write a note to you to get my mind straightened out again. I had intended to write to you this morning, having put it off too long.

You will soon be leaving for Cornish now that May has come. I am *so* glad you were here when Florence went. I can't tell you what a comfort you were all winter long to Florence and to me. We didn't talk to you *very* often, but the thought that you were at the other end of a telephone wire, and that you were thinking of Florence, and that we could see you from time to time, helped enormously. Florence did so enjoy your "visits"; they never tired her at all.

One of the worst aspects of her going is that I can no longer call her on the 'phone in the morning and be "bucked up" by her cheerfully sweet voice until I could get to her *ca.* 4:15 P.M. On Thursday morning at about 8:15, at the end of our little confab (in which she talked almost exclusively in monosyllables), I had the feeling for the first time that *she* felt she was to leave me soon. I ended with "I mustn't tire you—goodbye." She replied, slowly, "Good-bye—Sweet-heart." They were her last words to me. Less than five hours later she sank into a coma. The next morning [at 6:59 o'clock, April 24] she went away.

To the visit with her in the afternoon and evening, until a bit after ten, when she would fall asleep, I looked forward *all* day; it was heavenly just to be sitting beside her, even if she napped; and we had so much *fun* together, talking and reading and discussing the books. . . . .

Wasn't she a *heavenly* person? The sweetness of her smile, of her voice, of her thoughtfulness; the brilliance of her mind; her interest in everyone and everything; her practical competence—all these and a *thousand* other abilities and accomplishments made her what for years I called her: *The Incomparable Lady.*

If I had not loved her so long and so deeply, the ache now would not be so piercing—but I would not have it otherwise. To have been loved by her (and she *did* and *does* love me) and to have been married to her for even a few years, to *know* that I made her almost as happy as she made me during the last seven years of her sojourn in this sphere, to have been so *completely companionable* with anyone on this earth—this is my triumph forever. How many have had wives comparable to her and been happy in equal degree? Certainly *very* few.

There was never anything humdrum or dull in our life together. There was but one capacity (that most people have) which she lacked: that for being bored. She was the antithesis of *Hedda Gabler.* Last Sunday evening Dr. Vogt, during his call, said, somewhat hesitantly: "I suppose, after her interesting life in China and elsewhere abroad, she must have found life in America a *little* dull sometimes." I had never thought of that with respect to her, but, instantly, I replied that he was *wrong, completely* wrong: she was never bored or dull and never pined to be where she wasn't. She could hardly understand my homesickness at times for China (part of which was based on the marvelous time we had together in 1938–39) . . . . and remarked sometimes that she was content to live wherever she had her work and it was necessary for her to live. Climate, sunshine (for which latter I pine in the winter months), etc., meant little or nothing to her. She was not mercurial and cared not at all whether the day were dark or bright, dry or wet. I react to the weather—and am *so thankful* that she left me on a beautiful day at the height of spring; that the services for her, here and in Boston, were on perfect days. . . . .

The committal service in Boston [at which our old friend, Dr. Francis Lister Hawks Pott, president emeritus of St. John's University, officiated] took place at 12:30 P.M. (by "accident" the hour of our marriage ceremony) on Wednesday [April 29]. The day was fine. I will sometime tell you more of it, if you care to have me. Now, I have written at too great length. Enough for the present.

To me, one of the most satisfying of Florence's writings is her essay on Li Ch'ing-chao, "whom," as she states in *Chinese Women: Yesterday and Today*, "the Chinese consider their greatest poetess." If you have read it, I am sure you remember it; if you have not, you will wish to do so. I do not believe that Florence could have composed it at any other period than that in which she did. As truly as did the Chinese, so admired by her, who use the brush to depict life's movement, in poetry, painting, or calligraphy, did Florence herself portray life's movement, and particularly her own personality, by the use of the pen. It may be true, as she remarks, in her analysis of the subjects just mentioned, in the compendium entitled *China* (University of California Press, 1946) that "it is not to be doubted that in the brush the Chinese possess a medium denied to us" and that "the Chinese artist pours out his soul from the soft hair tip on the slender bamboo tube"; but no less true is it that she, distilling the essence of her own beauty of soul and life-experience, found in pen and ink and fir-flower paper a means of expressing beauty, life, faith, and love for the ages. And in her published writings, nowhere else is there to be found a better example of her ability to do this than in her appreciation of Li Ch'ing-chao.

When the time came to choose from Florence's writings a quotation to be cut on the stone in Forest Hills Cemetery, I selected one of the final observations by the great poetess in her Preface to the *Chin Shih Lu* ("Record of Golden Stones"), from Florence's translation:

> To have the have one must suffer the not have; those
> who rejoice in union must endure separation. This
> universal law is the Rule of Life.

And I join with Li Ch'ing-chao in her final statement: "My slight record, from end to opening, is a warning to the learned, the accomplished, to all in this floating world who love ancient things. I close."

Most sincerely yours,

HARLEY FARNSWORTH MACNAIR

THE HOUSE OF THE WU-T'UNG TREES
5533 WOODLAWN AVENUE
CHICAGO 37, ILLINOIS
THE SEASON, SPRING
THE YEAR: 1946

PAULINUS TO AUSONIUS

Translated from the Latin by HELEN WADDELL

I, THROUGH all chances that are given to mortals
   And through all fates that be,
So long as this close prison shall contain me,
   Yea, though a world shall sunder me and thee,

Thee shall I hold, in every fibre woven,
   Not with dumb lips nor with averted face
Shall I behold thee, in my mind embrace thee,
   Instant and present, thou, in every place.

Yea, when the prison of this flesh is broken,
   And from the earth I shall have gone my way,
Wheresoe'er in the wide universe I stay me,
   There shall I bear thee, as I do to-day.

Think not the end, that from my body frees me,
   Breaks and unshackles from my love to thee.
Triumphs the soul above its house in ruin,
   Deathless, begot of immortality.

Still must she keep her senses and affections,
   Hold them as dear as life itself to be,
Could she choose death, then might she choose for-
     getting.
   Living, remembering, to eternity.

—*The Wandering Scholars*, pp. 10–11

PART II

YOUTH[1]

YOUTH is not a time of life; it is a state of mind . . . . it is a temper of the will, a quality of the imagination, a vigor of the emotions. It is the freshness of the deep springs of life.

Youth means a temperamental predominance of courage over timidity, of the appetite for adventure over the love of ease. . . . . Nobody grows old by merely living a number of years. People grow old only by deserting their ideals. Years wrinkle the skin; but to give up enthusiasm wrinkles the soul.

Worry, doubt, self-distrust, fear, and despair—these are the long, long years that bow the heart and turn the greening spirit back to dust. Whether sixty or sixteen, there is in every human being's heart the lure of wonder, the sweet amazement at the stars and at starlike things and thoughts, the undaunted challenge of events, the unfailing, childlike appetite for what next, and the joy of the game of living. You are as young as your faith, as old as your doubt; as young as your self-confidence, as old as your fear; as young as your hope, as old as your despair.

In the central place of your heart is an evergreen tree; its name is Love. So long as it flourishes, you are young. When it dies, you are old. In the central place of your heart is a wireless station. So long as it receives messages of beauty, hope, cheer, grandeur, courage, and power from God and from your fellowmen, so long are you young.—AUTHOR UNKNOWN.

[1] A friend wrote to Florence: "I am writing this on the back of a card which I like very much and thought you also might enjoy reading it." Florence mailed the card to me in a letter sent in August, 1935, while I was en route to Guernsey.

OF HERSELF SHE WROTE: EXCERPTS
FROM HER LETTERS

[*From Vienna, in 1930 to Lucille Douglass:*] I AM making no plans
but am just trying to make the most of things as they offer here—
am studying German . . . . and am now beginning to read
Chinese with a sinologist. . . . . My dear, I am so glad about
your success. I always *knew* that the lecture field was one for you;
didn't I always say so! It is grand that all is going so well in that
line. . . . . Am so interested to hear of Mei Lan-fang's success
[in America]—and am glad. He is an artist.

About the Chinese gardens' negatives—of course all I have is
yours, but how to get at what you want! Because, of course,
pictures and negatives are all in St. Andrews. . . . .

My dear, all you say about my work is so true—the whole
trouble lies in myself. . . . . If I were different, I suppose that I
could make some arrangement . . . . and go on with my work—.
As I am, I suppose that [to paraphrase Tu Fu] I shall go on
striving . . . . until my coffin is closed. . . . .

[*From Kurhotel, Gmunden, Salzkammergut, Austria, July 10, 1930,
to Ada Russell:*] You will be amused at me, but, having now taken
on the life of a gypsy—the very last I would have chosen—I
mean to make the most of its advantages and to try to enjoy living in one room with very little of my own about me. It is funny
the way Fate deals cards one would *not* choose. After all, life is
like a game of cards, to use a rather unoriginal simile—one must
just make the best of the hand that turns up and try to win out
on it. . . . .

I can see you in a cool dress among your flowers. Did those I
sent grow? I wonder whether I shall ever have my own flower
beds again? In any case, I have *had* them. No one can take away
what one has enjoyed. . . . . and think of me as the gypsy. I can
assure you the gypsies "have nothing on me." When the caravan
stops, out comes everything imaginable and before long I am

"chez moi." I wish you could see my folding desk and chair! A marvel!! It is time to go down and swim. . . . . It is very lovely on the Traun Lake.

[*From Gmunden, Austria, August 11, 1930, to Ada Russell:*] To me my home has always been the most precious thing that there was . . . . one's home must be a place where harmony reigns, where one can express one's self, where one can talk quietly with one's friends. . . . . Yes, my dear, I love the Island [in Passamaquoddy Bay, near St. Andrews] very much. . . . . I do love it. Curious how different different scenery is. I am try- ing—with signal unsuccess—to try to understand the mountains. I feel as if I could not endure never to see the sun set! Having lived all my life either on a vast plain or by the sea, the sight of these huge rocks all about me fills me with awe and a certain dis- comfort. . . . . It is funny to be living like a gypsy, but I wish that you could see my "outfit." I have two little plants that travel with me "where e'er I go." Nice substitute for the Island, the orchard, and the perennial border. . . . .

[*On board the "Jean de Breyde," crossing from Ostend to Dover, January 13, 1931 to H. F. M.:*] My typewriter is perched on a table improvised from life-preservers and sofa cushions; my person is perched on the knife-edge of a sofa; my little car is tucked in a tarpaulin on the after-deck. . . . . The gypsy caravan en route for America. . . . .

[*From Philadelphia, March 12, 1931, to H. F. M.:*] My earliest ambition was to be a circus rider. I feel—although I am not clad in pink tulle, nor have I any stout white horse—that this ambition has been, figuratively speaking, fulfilled. I spring through the hoop of Court Life into the T'ang Dynasty at Philadelphia Museum this afternoon. . . . .

[*From 22 Hauteville, Guernsey, Channel Islands, August 17, 1931, to H. F. M.:*] . . . . I have indeed bought a house here and shall be busy settling in. . . . . The house—it is very different from any other house I have ever had—is the other half of the one inhabited by Victor Hugo's *chère amie.* . . . . We look over the harbor, a most interesting and amusing view . . . . across the bay to the islands of Herm, Jethou, and Sark, and then away to France. A marvelous view. . . . .

I had to leave Yo Fei in Vienna. It seems to me that a part of myself has been left behind; and it is almost so. For nearly thirteen years he has been my shadow and I have been his slave. Dear little dog.

Am now preparing to go to the Orientalists' Congress in Leyden. . . . .

Oh, you will be amused. The Fox Film people made a tone film of me writing Chinese characters and talking about them (in German) just before I left Vienna. It *was* a piece of work, *so* difficult. . . . .

[*November 22, 1933:*] . . . . I note what you say, or what you rather repeat,[1] in regard to an autobiographical book from my pen, which you are kind enough to want to read, but the simple fact is—and please do not think that I am falsely modest when I say—the simple fact is that I am far more interested in Tu Fu's Autobiography than I am in my own.

[*New Year's Day, 1935: At the Grass Hut on the Yellow Reach, Shanghai, to Ada Russell:*] . . . . I am such an utterly abandoned correspondent! Did only the interviews I have with my friends transfer themselves from my brain to paper—automatically— what a lot you would hear! Because, you see, I think of my friends very, very often—and last night as I stood on a little stool waiting to jump into the new year—a ceremony I always observe—I made a mental journey around the globe and looked in upon you all.

. . . . I adore turning back the clock of time—let who will look forward. I find joy in the mist of days gone by.

[*From western Pennsylvania, while motoring eastward, June 21, 1935, to H. F. M.:*] *Pleasantville*—formerly called *Dubstown!!!* Think, however, I would rather live in honest Dubstown than self-conscious Pleasantville. We are floating through the mountains of western Pennsylvania. I use the word "floating" with

[1] Earlier, F. A. wrote to H. F. M.: "If the book you urge me to write is ever done, it shall *certainly* be dedicated to you."

intention. We seem actually to float from one hill top to the next. . . . . Shut in the Tan Jaguar [the motorcar] we seem to have dropped from some other planet. . . . . Oh! I wonder what is going to happen? Never have I seen such a "lucky group"— a hay wagon stood by a field full of sheep *to our left*—opposite field full of lucky pigs. What say you to that?

[*Near the U.S.–Canadian frontier, July 10, 1935, to H. F. M.:*] Breasted's book [*The Dawn of Conscience*] . . . . moves me deeply. Please read it. On the title-page he quotes a sentence from Emerson to the effect that our civilization is only at its cock-crow and its morning star, that character is only in its infancy. Emerson reached his conclusion through intuition. Breasted evolves his from the basis of historical and archeological fact. He expresses what I felt dimly at the Grand Canyon when the young man spoke. He enunciates that which I believe with my whole being: I mean that Man is a moral being; that he has, through the ages, evolved a conscience; that, being human, he is divine; that his spiritual development has an amazing future; that our responsibility to ourselves is infinite. . . . .

[*On board the R.M.S. "Duchess of Richmond," July 11, 1935, to H. F. M.:*] Did it amuse you to hear me through the air last night? It amused me very much. I do love feeling the thrill of modern science. The "magic" of man's control.

[*On board the R.M.S. "Duchess of Richmond," in the St. Lawrence, July 12, 1935, to H.F.M.:*] Do you remember . . . . I once told you that life seemed to me a brocade strip? Each one of us is given a length to weave and the patterns we make gain in values by their contrasts. Each pattern must be rounded out—here, or perhaps in the life to come. Tu Fu said: "I am impatient—*very!*" I resemble him, and often try to hurry my weaving. The threads then tangle, and I grieve.

[*In the St. Lawrence, July 13, 1935 to H. F. M.:*] Trees, you know, are a passion with me, so we have much to talk about. . . . .

[*At sea, July 16, 1935, to H. F. M.:*] . . . . I fell upon Cranmer-Byng's *Vision of Asia* which *must* be reviewed before I leave the ship. . . . . It contains many very fine thoughts. . . . . "This is the beginning of adventure—to become the world we live in, the very spirit of our time . . . . to draw all streams and tributaries to ourselves." That is *fine*. I think that I have said to you that my only dread of old age is that it tends to make people static, unelastic, intolerant of unaccustomed ideas. Each generation has its voice. I want to try and hear the voices of those younger than I. With Cranmer-Byng's thesis I—and I *know you* agree—am in fullest accord. East and West must comprehend each other —must join to form a world civilization. . . . . Tonight the inevitable ship's concert—only stern duty takes one to that . . . . [*July 17:*] Ship's concert surprisingly good. In one "sketch" the performer referred to "the sort of woman who puts on her clothes with a bad aim." I thought that that would appeal to you!

Cranmer-Byng is dealt with. . . . . Do you remember this passage? "For Huai Nantze has been careful to define what is meant by 'inaction.' It is not, as some scholars seem to think, 'doing nothing.' It is rather the doctrine of the right opportunity, of acting on the inevitable hour, of striking the timely note that passes into harmony with others and produces a perfect chord. Those who are called inactive are such as do not attempt to force things with premature action."—Good.

[*From 22 Hauteville, Guernsey, August 12, 1935, to H. F. M.:*] . . . . Guernsey is at its loveliest self, and I plunge into the deep-green sea every day; am trying to make myself "very fit." . . . .

[*From Chicago, December 9, 1935, to Ada Russell:*] . . . . You ask of me—Ada dear. I am so happy that it frightens me. I cannot write more. On January 15 I am to speak in New York for the Women Geographers. . . . . My love, Ada dearest—life is full of emotion.

[*From the House of the Wu-t'ung Trees, Chicago, July 20, 1940, to Ada Russell:*] . . . . Life here is full and most interesting. People are charming to me, and I do all sorts of things which I enjoy. This summer, for instance, I am giving a course of public lectures at the University on Chinese life as reflected in art, literature,

IN THE HOUSE OF THE WU-T'UNG TREES
By one of the illuminated doors of the Chinese cabinet

etc.[2] Rather a topic? eh? I begin with *Homo erectus pekinensis* and continue to the present. . . . . In October, I am going to speak on Amy [Lowell] at the Harriet Monroe Poetry Room in the University. . . . . Once a month there are meetings, and it is at the first of these that I plan to speak. I shall show the slides of Sevenels which were shown at the Keats House. . . . .

[2] Announced by the University of Chicago as follows:

CHINESE SOCIETY AS REFLECTED IN LITERATURE, THE ARTS, FOLKLORE, AND HANDICRAFT

A Series of Twelve Illustrated Lectures by
Florence Ayscough, Litt.D. (Mrs. Harley Farnsworth MacNair)
Author and Lecturer in Chinese Literature and Art
3:30 p.m. on Tuesdays and Thursdays, Social Science Research Assembly Room

FIRST TERM. FROM PREHISTORIC DAYS TO THOSE OF SOUTHERN SUNG

June 25 and 27. Paleolithic to 206 B.C.: "From the Days of *Homo erectus pekinensis* to the Rise of the Han Dynasty"

July 2 and 9. 206 B.C. to A.D. 618: "Rise of the Han Dynasty to Rise of the T'ang"

July 11 and 16. A.D. 618–1127: "Rise of the T'ang Dynasty to Fall of the Northern Sung"

SECOND TERM. FROM THE DAYS OF SOUTHERN SUNG TO THE PRESENT

July 30 and August 1. A.D. 1127–1644: "Days of the Southern Sung Dynasty to the Rise of Ch'ing, the Manchu Dynasty"

August 6, 8, 13, and 15. A.D. 1644–1940: "Rise of the Ch'ing Dynasty to the Present Day"

LISTEN TO THE EXHORTATION OF THE DAWN!

Look well to this day! For it is life—
The very life of life—
In its brief course lie all the verities
And realities of your existence—
The bliss of growth,
The glory of action,
The splendour of beauty.
For yesterday is but a dream,
And tomorrow is only a vision.
But today well lived
Makes every yesterday a dream of happiness,
And every tomorrow a vision of hope.
Look well, therefore, to this day!
Such is the salutation of the dawn.

—FROM THE SANSKRIT
(Copied for H. F. M. by F. A. M.)

OF HER IT WAS WRITTEN WHILE
SHE WAS HERE

ABOUT FLORENCE AYSCOUGH
(who wrote the book)

By LUCILLE DOUGLASS
(who drew the pictures)[1]

WE SAT in Florence Ayscough's upstairs study at St. Andrews, in New Brunswick, looking through the broad window laced with branches, across the Bay of Plentiful Fish. I had found her there at her desk, a vivid picture in scarlet and purple—the colours which she has made peculiarly her own and of which she has woven brilliant patterning across her allotted space in the tapestry of life. Her profile showed clear-cut against the dark frame of a mirror in which was reflected the brilliant green of the leaves outside, dancing in the sunlight. The necklace of opals she wore sent back this brightness in myriad shafts of colour, making a perfect setting for the portrait I had come to paint. The colours fairly sang—the colours on my palette answered, but over my soul settled the shadow of utter inadequacy. "Ah," I exclaimed, paraphrasing Li T'ai-po, who has referred to "the bitterness of writing poetry," "I feel the bitterness of painting portraits."

One can put on canvas the finely modelled features, carved in broad planes, as if sculptured from marble; the black hair, with its peculiar dusky purple quality, folding itself into a frame for the face, but it is another matter to fix the lightning shift of expression that harmonizes with her quickly moving mind—like the play of light and shade on the surface of the mirror.

Before my eyes rose innumerable pictures against innumerable backgrounds. In place of the mirror and its gay reflections, I saw her sitting in front of the Moon Fireplace in her Grass Hut on the Yellow Reach, where so often I sat literally at her feet and listened while she read her newest translation or talked of the

[1] Being part of the Introduction (pp. ix–xiii) to *Firecracker Land: Pictures of the Chinese World for Younger Readers* (New York: Junior Literary Guild and Houghton Mifflin Co., 1932).

Chinese culture which forms the background of her life. Sometimes it was the theatre of which she is so fond and which we often attended together, accompanied by the Number Two Boy, who translated for us. Again, it was the intimate happenings of the household—for Mrs. Ayscough always takes the keenest interest in all those who touch her life, however casually. Her range of interests ran the gamut from the larger concerns of war relief to the home for Chinese girls who were salvaged from unspeakable misery and hardship and cared for until suitable marriages could be arranged for them. She is peculiarly sympathetic with young people.

One incident comes vividly to my mind. Pavlova was giving a series of performances in Shanghai. Mrs. Ayscough had a birthday party for me, taking us later to see the famous dancer. Pavlova was impersonating the French doll. Looking at her exquisite dance, it seemed to me such a pity to be grown up and disillusioned, and I said to Mrs. Ayscough: "When I see that, I long to be ten years old. How I wish every child in Shanghai could watch that doll come to life. It would be like seeing a miracle."

Instantly her face lit up. "They *shall* see it!" she exclaimed.

No sooner said than done. An early morning visit to Pavlova. A conference with the manager of the theatre. A matinee was arranged. The schools were notified. The house was filled with eager faces. The curtain went up and the miracle happened. When the curtain fell in the last number, there was a great sigh—but for a little space the children had dwelt in paradise.

In the years that I have known Florence Ayscough, I have many times been puzzled that she is so deeply rooted in the Far East, with so complete an understanding of the ancient Chinese thought and culture as if she were one with them. This is all the more strange because her ancestors were of New England stock. It is very unusual that an Occidental is so at home in Oriental processes of thought—just as if they spoke the same language. Not only does she understand them, but is able in her writings to make others understand them, which in itself is a rare gift.

Mrs. Ayscough writes of China from within; putting into her vivid telling not only the pageantry of that age-old country, for she has traveled from east to west and from north to south the roads of ancient culture, but describing with a deep conviction the customs and manners, the religious teachings and cults. . . . .

The problems of China which are confronting the world today will still confront the world of tomorrow; they are the heritage of the next generation. So any light that can be thrown upon them is of vital importance. In this book for young people, Mrs. Ayscough has given generously of her wealth of knowledge of Chinese culture. From her years of study and travel she has woven a rich tapestry against which the events of today and tomorrow can be seen in sharp relief. . . . .

I feel a close kinship with *A Chinese Mirror* and [*Firecracker Land:*] *Pictures of the Chinese World*, for it has been in this collaboration, if an illustrator may so dignify her work, that I have been brought into close contact with Mrs. Ayscough. It has given me, too, a new insight into her many-sided character; one phase especially, that might be called the keynote—an absolutely undeviating devotion to the truth. This unswerving loyalty on her part and my artistic impressionism often brought me in sharp contact with unexpected corners. This same divergence of viewpoint was introduced when I was painting the slides[2] for her lecture on Tu Fu. I looked at them from the pictorial angle, she from the point of the incident she wished to illustrate. She is a very artistic as well as competent photographer, which enables her to record the exact place desired for the slide, and prefers, if possible, to use her own photographs for her lectures.

Her whole attitude toward life is constructive; she attacks a building problem[3] with the same buoyant enthusiasm with which she approaches a new literary task, and does it as thoroughly. In the building of The Grass Hut by the Yellow Reach in Shanghai, she followed to the smallest detail the ceremonies used by the Chinese in the construction of a Kiangsu [province] farmhouse. . . . . [And, in an article for the *Boston Evening Transcript*, Miss Douglass added:]

. . . . I find myself striving to probe into her inner conscious-

[2] Presented, in 1946 with most of the collection of her slides, to the China Society of America, New York.

[3] When plans were being drawn up in Shanghai for an addition to the St. Andrews, New Brunswick, home, their success depended upon a correct estimation by F. A. of the width of a staircase in that home. On the arrival of the plans in Canada, it was found that the estimation was within two inches of the actuality.

ness in order to find the corresponding chord—the will to understand a foreign process of thought—a will often so curiously lacking in Occidentals. There is, too, the unexpected adaptability, a deep understanding which enables her to reproduce perfectly an alien civilization—its faults and weaknesses as well as its glory and strength. . . . .

Not all of Mrs. Ayscough's time is given to writing. Her lectures play an important role in her interpretation of the life of the Far East. These lectures had their inception in the work at the Royal Asiatic Library in Shanghai. After the beginning of the World War, in 1916, the British Chamber of Commerce organized a language school for young business men; a consular official who was much interested in it asked her to make a list of books that should be read by people studying Chinese subjects and talk to the students about them. She said, "Why I couldn't; I could never lecture."

"Well, if you can't you can't, I suppose," replied the official, "but you jolly well should be able to." There was no gainsaying the truth of this assertion, so the plunge was taken, and since then Mrs. Ayscough has lectured before many distinguished audiences in many countries, America, China, Japan [Germany, Austria, Sweden, Canada], England and France. . . . .

Scholar, musician [at times guest artist with the Shanghai Municipal Orchestra], artist, and poet, but most of all a gracious woman, whose enthusiasm for life makes radiant all who come her way and whose humanity reaches out to others in complete understanding. It is so I have painted her portrait, the Opalescent Lady.

FLORENCE AYSCOUGH[1]

In a recent issue of the *New York Herald-Tribune*, James W. Bennett, who knows his China well, and who is the author of several books dealing with China through the medium of the story, tells of those who, regarded by the unknown as alien in their thoughts and desires, have nevertheless contributed to the greater understanding between the Chinese and foreigners.

"Old China Hands" is the title of Mr. Bennett's article, and he shows clearly that the name, apparently a derisive term, has, however, a gentler and more endearing interpretation to those who are familiar with the trend of Chinese thought and affairs. Among the men and women, chosen to represent this idea are a diplomat; a banker; an enthusiastic advocate of that elusive ideal, the brotherhood of man, who died of weariness and blasted hopes; two missionaries, one a medical man and the other a teacher in a girls' school who was killed in a riot. Their stories ended, Mr. Bennett writes:

"It is with some relief that I turn to another 'Old China Hand' of the softer, more charming sex. With her the adjective 'Old' is distinctly ungracious, for in spite of the encroaching years she has kept her youth and enthusiasms. With that enthusiasm has gone a hard, exacting scholarship which has resulted in several unusual books. . . . . She has delved into an ancient lore and patiently tried to show the philosophic currents and cross-currents that make up the great stream of Chinese thought today. As she says:

" 'China is usually treated by the West from a purely academic point of view; that is, her art, literature and archaeology are studied as are similar subjects with dead civilizations; but China is alive, and she is virile; moreover, her ancient beliefs and thoughts are indissolubly knit into the life of her people.'

"It is," concludes Mr. Bennett, "before Florence Ayscough, co-author with Amy Lowell of that magnificent translation of the Chinese poets, *Fir-Flower Tablets;* as author of *A Chinese Mir-*

[1] From the editorial page of the *Telegraph-Journal*, St. John, N.B., February 20, 1931.

ror, that I should like to lay my small chaplet. She is the quintessence, the finest flowering of the Old China Hand.''

Praise that cannot fail to interest Mrs. Ayscough's own countrymen here in New Brunswick, where because of the proverb concerning a prophet and his own people there has been a slower appreciation of her genius than in the East and in England. However, all things come to those who wait—and read—and the full flowering of her acclaim will be the Indian summer of the next generation.

YIN-YANG

By MAUDE MEAGHER[1]

As THE reflection of torches in a dark sea;
As the bright incalculable pennons of flame
about their night-blue core;
As the slow roots that reach into the unhurried
remembering earth;
In the lightless essence of death—that is, life—
comprehended,
SO YIN.

As the bright arch of the sky above the reaching
branches of trees;
As the sparkling of sun on the constant and
various sea;
As the changing light on the rocks,
purple shadows and scarlet fire—
SO YANG.

[1] Written by M. M. in autographing for F. A., in 1932, a copy of *Fantastic Traveller*. Copied for H. F. M. by F. A. on a Fir-Flower Tablet. In the upper left corner of the Tablet appear the characters *Sung Ch'ing* ("Pine Tree Elf"), the name given by F. A. to M.M. In the upper right corner appears the character *Ai* ("Love"), part of F. A.'s Chinese name. The three characters were written by F. A. The following note also appears: "The Elf always feels that she exemplifies Yin—& that I exemplify Yang."

TO HER IT WAS WRITTEN

FLORENCE DEAR, this is just to tell you, what you know quite well already, that I think of you all the time and wish it were possible to know daily how things are going. . . . . He must begrudge every moment he has to spend away from you.

I have been thankful through all this for your philosophy and serenity of spirit; these must have helped you, as I am sure they have those about you.

No one can put as much color into life. It wouldn't surprise me if you could make an adventure, even of being ill.

You would be amused to see Mrs. Bissell and me taking a Red Cross first-aid course. . . . . Next week we were told to bring blankets so we could lie prostrate on the floor and have artificial respiration applied to us, besides applying it to others!! You, who attacked both the stove and the automobile without hesitation, would, I suppose, regard this without trepidation, but it is not so, alas, with me. I shall think of *your* way of approach to this, and, I hope, other things that—are really important.

. . . . I miss you *very* much and, though I know I am only one of many, I just wanted to tell you again how much you mean to me, Florence dear, Yours, ADELA [BARRETT], Chicago.

Often you have been in my thoughts, and I have wished that I could do something to brighten the hours in bed, for we all miss you, dear Mrs. MacNair, and are so eager to have you in our midst. We need just those rare, lovely qualities of thought that you always express. . . . .—FLORENCE DIBELL BARTLETT, Chicago.

I was reading *Tu Fu* the other day, nostalgically longing for China, and, as always when I read what you have written, I wanted to tell you how marvelously poignant you have made that dynasty and the life of a poet. With your splendid scholarship you have given such precious things to us—to us who are on the outer edge of China, loving the country and the people, yet unable to penetrate to the intellectual core of life. . . . .
—DOROTHY GRAHAM BENNETT, New York.

. . . . the delightful memory of the interesting talk you gave to the decorators last year—it was so generous of you to give so much of yourself, and I assure you that it was appreciated. I think, very often, of how good you were to help me that day—and of how untiringly you worked for the Chinese Relief. It has been an inspiration to me, and I want to thank you again. . . . . —NINA BINGHAM, Chicago.

Did you ever hear her famous compliment about you? You gave the school children [of St. Andrews, N.B.] tickets for a lecture, where you introduced the speaker. Alexie came home; the lecture was nice—but "Mrs. Ayscough was beautiful. She wore a lovely blue velvet dress. She looked just like Queen Victoria." Bless her heart! Gen and I never even smiled.—FREDA W. BISHOP, St. Andrews, N.B., and Peoria, Ill.

I know of no one who brings such a combination of almost fairy gifts to her work. Most of us would be contented with one: birth and life in a country rich and strange, or poetic intelligence, or creative ability, or opportunities for world travel, or contact with the world's great ones—you have them all. Your life has always had (to use a much-abused word) glamour, hasn't it? —J. S. B., Chicago.

You do bring us something especially lovely and inspiring each time, and we are hoping you will be back with us very soon. —MABEL COOK COLE, Chicago.

You have spurred me on to further study and investigation of the fascinating legends and superstitions connected with our old city here, and I may really do something with them sometime. I have toyed with the thought of writing up and locating by maps and pictures these old spots and temples and seeing if I could find a publisher who would be interested. I'd be glad to know what you would think about it? I shall do it for my own pleasure anyway, but it might, in view of Nanking's new prominence, be of interest to others.—H. D. D., Nanking.

Such joy—such intense pleasure as you gave us [of the Poetry Group, Shanghai] this morning [June 12, 1939]—is just *beyond* my most adequate(?) powers to express—perhaps the sales of your book may show it to the extent of 11 copies at least!!

And may I add—that if at any time you—tho' I can't imagine it—tire of book writing—you might as successfully take up the Stage—"play acting" such as *you* did this morning, just picking us up out of war tensions and realism that defies anything one has *ever* heard of or read—and transporting us to the very heart of old Cathay—takes peculiar genius—and *that* type is *yours*. Strangely enough, Bertha Jaques writes—got it tonight—after the MacNairs.

Please accept the sincere thanks of Poetry Group and ELLA ELY.

Since your most charming program at our Woman's Club, I have thought of you frequently. . . . . I hope you have some deep sense of personal satisfaction after such a program as compensation for the great enjoyment which you pass on to your audience. . . . . Besides the subject matter—which was most fascinating —you pass on to us so much of your own personality that we are carried out of ourselves and forgetting our inhibitions and problems and lacks—become, for the time we are listening, a part of your larger world of experience and appreciation. That is why my mother and I walked a mile twice a week to your summer lectures [1940], which were our only summer vacation in a rather bad summer for us otherwise—they will be all that we shall remember of it. . . . .—MIRIAM LIBBY EVANS, Chicago.

There is a richness of experience about you that, although we touched it but lightly, we found so very unusual and so stimulating. One of the unforgettable evenings, for me, was that night you asked us to dinner and read some of your poetry to us after dinner. Perhaps you have read it many times, but I cannot help but think that, in the setting of your own home, surrounded by evidences of your life in China, something was added to that reading.—NELLIE D. FAIRWEATHER, Barrington.

I send this little plant to bring my love and to say that I am not only *re*-reading your book, *Chinese Women*, which you autographed for Mrs. Biller, for me, but also on my walls, just framed, is the "Reward of Recognition" signed by Mme Chiang. So you see that not only you but your beloved China is also in my heart. . . . . I loved your Christmas card with its shadows of the trees in your yard behind the Chinese cabinets—that, too, is in my own room!—Addie Hibbard Gregory, Chicago.

It isn't fun to be ill, but you are a plucky person and a gay one. God bless you for it. . . . . Dear Florence, it *was* such a joy to have seen you—may we soon meet again.—Lisa Grierson, Boston.

I am only reiterating this morning what not only I said to you but what I heard the others who listened to your delightful and illuminating talk last evening—that you gave us pleasure and profit of knowledge—and zest to know more. . . . . Today, when . . . . our sympathies are with China, it was indeed refreshing to hear you speak about a cultural side of China.—Carrie M. Hales, Oak Park.

This morning the sun was shining in our windows when I woke up, and I remembered that paragraph in Cronin's *The Keys of the Kingdom:* "Waking in the morning with the starlings chattering in the eaves, and the coolness of the dawn still dewed upon the grass; his second thought was that there could be no greater happiness than to work—much with the hands, a little with the head, but mostly with his heart—and to live like this, close to the earth which, to him, never seemed far from heaven." I no more than thought of that passage when it seemed to me it described you, except that you work *much* with your head as well as much with your hands which created that beautiful home where we all love to gather. As for your heart, not a soul meets you who doesn't feel its warmth and kindness. And you and Harley have made a lovely garden where you and your friends can be close to the earth. . . . .—Janet Harvey, Chicago.

Many happy returns of the day and all the love in the world. It is too bad I cannot be near you, for I would love so to sit and have a good *chat.* You are such a stimulating person and I need bucking up terribly, mentally. . . . . You are so wonderful, just an inspiration to us all. . . . . I wish you could be a fly on the wall at my first-aid course. . . . . One woman asked if one began artificial respiration after rigor mortis set in. Another was asked what to do in an accident where a man had lost a foot. She said, "Try and make him forget it." . . . . Do you remember when Nita was born and I was so ill and could not seem to get my strength back? When we . . . . cabled you to be godmother—your immediate loving cable seemed to give me strength and courage. If I only could do the same for you now. You have always been my ideal, and if you only knew how hard I have tried to be kind and understanding to servants and dependents and animals as you are.—You are everything that is finest and best and the most splendid, clear-minded person I ever knew. —ANITA HINCKLEY, Providence, R.I.

I have deliberately refrained from writing or bothering you or adding to your burdens in any way, hoping, for the time when I could call and see your smiling face. . . . . You are always in my mind.—MARY E. KAUFMAN, Chicago.

We are missing you so much at the Bank. Your lovely smile and, better still, that indefinable something about you which always leaves us feeling a bit happier and a bit more encouraged to carry on our own job is a stimulus that we need.
All that I can say is—that it is economically and socially wrong for "You" to be out of circulation for so long a period.
We just want you to know how very much we are missing you. With love and appreciation.—M. ELIZABETH KROUSE, Chicago.

These flowers are not from China, and, alas, I am too deficient in botany to recall whether they could even be remotely paralleled in China. But I hope that they will bring to you a little of my appreciation of what you mean to all lovers of China and, particularly, to this one.—KENNETH S. LATOURETTE, Yale University.

How we wish you were with us! The fresh charm of a Chinese lily opening in the large window at the College Club gives a fragrant reminder of your radiant personality. Warm love and good wishes.—MARJORIE B. LEAVENS, Chicago.

Your smile has brought cheer into our neighborhood ever since you have been here, and we hope you will be back soon. A beautiful ice storm which would add to the Christmas greeting you sent in 1940, and which I treasure as a work of art and joy forever.—CAROLINE W. MONTGOMERY, Chicago.

So often this winter I have thought of that first year you came to New York with your Chinese paintings and how many happy times we had together looking at them and studying them and the day you took me to Mr. Simkhovich, where we saw that beautiful Hsia Kuei that still gives me the greatest pleasure. . . . .—ADA S. MOORE, New York.

Speaking of fog, I have a lovely example of native wit to tell you. An old fisherman was telling a tourist how thick the fog was here. He said it was so thick that once, when he was shingling a barn, he could not see when he came to the edge and kept right on nailing the shingles on the fog. When the tourist seemed skeptical, he said he could prove it—for some people on the islands had noticed the nail holes in the fog as it drifted out.

The Tea House did very well last summer. . . . . We did not bother you about giving us a deed of the building as it seems that one only needs a deed when land is involved. . . . . Anyway, everything is all right, and we are delighted to have the Tea House.—NELLIE MOWAT, St. Andrews, N.B.

How much you—and your beautiful work—have done to interest the world in China, and to create an understanding and appreciation of all that China means! . . . . You must be very proud of the magnificent fight that China has been—and is—putting up.—BLAIR NILES, New York.

. . . . and you have given us all such riches. I have all your books standing where I can reach out to them whenever I am in my Chinese study. You do not know how much I have used your books to inoculate my students with a knowledge and understanding of the richness and glory of Chinese life.

A young woman came to call upon me the other day and mentioned meeting you at the little dinner we had one night when you were with me in Boston and spoke to the girls. She has never forgotten your dog—and tea made from the drops of water from the lotus blossom. You have given so much inspiration and joy to so many eager hungry people, out of your inspired under-standing.

Last summer I was on the Pacific Coast and for a brief hour saw the girls [Maude Meagher and Caroline Smiley, editor and business manager, respectively, of *World Youth*, a periodical for the young of all ages] building their new home [Casa de Tierra, El Quito Road, Los Gatos, California]. . . . . It is lovely, snug and inviting; sits in an orchard of rich purple prune trees heavy with velvety fruit. As one lifts the eye, the wide valley and the far mountains bring a glowing picture of warm sun and beauty. . . . . I hope they find a way to success—they are a rare pair, and you and I are responsible for their having found each other. . . . .
—KATHERINE OSBORNE, Boston.

. . . . Apart from your rare treasures of Chinese art and their arrangement, you seem to me to have been particularly success-ful in building into your house the protective feeling of being wholly within it, which in modern house building has been mostly sacrificed to external "effects."—MARTIN SCHÜTZE, Chi-cago.

. . . . in some years of reading, and listening to travelers, never before have I known one who could so vividly give the feeling of an alien civilization to one who has never visited it.
—H. W. S., Chicago.

We just arrived home on the hills of Los Angeles; that is why I delayed up to this day to thank you for your letter of introduc-tion which opened the doors of *Asia* so easily that this magazine is soon going to reproduce four of my drawings on Indochina. Other doors in the University of Chicago are to be opened on your account. Mr. Middeldorf decided on December or January for the show.—J. VIGOUREUX, Los Angeles.

And I've been re-reading the Second volume of *Tu Fu*, perennial-ly delightful. It's a grand book. How I wish that you would translate another poet. All of Li T'ai-po, please; you would do it so much better than Obata. And Mêng Hao-Jen—only I'm not sure of the spelling. . . . .—FLORANCE WATERBURY, New York.

. . . . your so fruitful life, and your enthralling studies. I have given away almost all my books, but your *Tu Fu*'s are still among my most treasured possessions. I find it so refreshing to dip into the pages and see a peculiarly vivid bit of colour (but not more vivid than your own entirely unique photographs). Or bring away some great thought, packed in the smallest compass. . . . . I want to tell you, too, what deep interest those photographs [taken on the island of Guernsey] of the mother-goddess have awakened among my friends. I marvel that such crude carvings could radiate such terrible power. . . . . How I wish we could meet and talk! To be with you so soothes and stimulates.
—ETHEL ROLT WHEELER, London.

PART III

THINKING OF THE FRONTIER
By Li T'ai-po

There is white snow on the Western hills and the clouds of
Ch'in are dark.
It is three thousand *li* from here to the Jade Barrier.
I desire to send the "harmonious writings," but how can they
reach you?

— *Fir-Flower Tablets*, p. 63

IN NEW YORK, 1917—BY THE PAINTING FROM WHICH THE HOUSE OF
THE WU-T'UNG TREES DERIVED ITS NAME

Now in the Art Institute, Chicago

OF HER LAST TWO APPEARANCES IN PUBLIC

[On November 26, 1941, two days before F. A. M. entered the hospital, the House of the Wu-t'ung Trees was opened to a group from Evanston to aid China Relief. Of this occasion, the last on which F. A. M. gave a reading from Chinese poetry, one visitor wrote:]

I know that Mrs. Scott made our report to you and expressed our gratitude for the beautiful afternoon in your home. But I want to write myself to tell you that not only I but many of our friends hold that afternoon in our memories as a period of enchantment like none we ever had before! It was like something out of the *Arabian Nights*, some rich and gracious vision of Aladdin's Lamp. And your voice with its inimitable poetic inflection made the spell complete. I can *never* thank you sufficiently—and I am more happy than I can say that so many of those we asked have expressed the same sense of a fine and subtle beauty and harmony. . . . .

And let me thank you also for the rare experience of the [Han] "Clinic"[1]—I am certain your Poet was describing the very

[1] Ward Walker, in the *Chicago Tribune* for November 28, 1941, under the heading "Art of Ancient China Shown at Oriental Clinic," wrote:

"In a room at the Art Institute lined with objects that were young two thousand years ago, a small group of women and the institute's curator of oriental art, Charles Fabens Kelly, yesterday [November 27, 1941] held a clinic.

"All the art on display dated from the Han dynasty, 206 B.C.–A.D. 220—grotesque, potbellied images in bronze, exquisite jade scabbard buckles, and two sassy bronze dragons that were undoubtedly an ancient Chinese version of a Disney creation.

"A number of rubbings—made in much the same fashion as a child traces a coin head on a piece of paper—of statues and panels were also on display. They portray a number of weird monsters and certain symbolical items such as two trees with a common branch.

"Mrs. Harley F. MacNair, whose husband is professor of far eastern history at the University of Chicago, donated the rubbings. She told the legend behind the joined tree symbol:

" 'A wicked ruler desired the beautiful wife of a warrior. The warrior was sent into battle and killed, and the ruler had the woman carried to his castle.

" 'But the woman, so the legend has it, threw herself off the tower rather than submit to the ruler. In her girdle was pinned a note asking that she be buried in a common grave with her husband.

" 'The wicked ruler said No, and ordered them buried separately. Much to everyone's surprise, a tree grew out of each grave and the branches grew together—a symbol of everlasting love. . . . .' "

creatures and regions we saw in your rubbings and on the bronzes—and there again I have the feeling of having been allowed, like Alice, to enter with you through the same magic portal! With all my heart and imagination I thank you! Sincerely, ANNE GEORGE MILLAR, Evanston.

I have thought of you very, very often since I heard of your illness and have realized again and again what an unselfish act you did in coming down to talk to us the day of the Han clinic. I do hope that did not prove to have been too hard an ordeal, but, as is characteristic of you, I know you were then thinking of *others* and not yourself. . . . .—HELEN C. GUNSAULUS, Art Institute, Chicago.[2]

[2] In Peking, January, 1939, F. A. M. postponed for a few days a physical examination—which immediately preceded a surgical operation—because she had promised to give a lecture to the students of the Peking College of Chinese Studies and would not break an appointment at the last moment.

FROM THE HOSPITAL

[F. A. M. dictated the following telegram for Easter, 1942, to the Frank L. Hinckley cousins, Providence, Rhode Island:]

DEAR HINCKLEYS—root and branch: We think of you so much and appreciate your loving thoughts. The gorgeous red azalea is still a joy, and, today, comes its beautiful pink brother to carry on the beauty you send.

They tell me I am making splendid progress but the road seems long and hilly although smoothed by the loving attentions of Harley and many friends.

Happy Easter thoughts for you all.

FLORENCE

IT WAS always a pleasure to care for Mrs. MacNair. She never complained, and she always had something interesting to say. —MARY GANGER, R.N.

We often spoke of her, how kind and patient she was during her illness. . . . . It always seemed to me there was very little we could do for her. . . . . I often think of the times I'd open the door to visit her, and you were both so absorbed in your reading that I would not disturb you. She enjoyed that so very much and looked forward to your visits each day.—M. KERBS, Hospital Supervisor.

Although I had the slightest acquaintance with her, I knew her to be a very gracious and wonderful lady. She signed my scrapbook and wrote several words in Chinese in it, and I feel very honored to have her signature.

I watched for her to go by my door each morning [in the hospital] and missed her greeting when she was no longer able to go down the hall.

I shall always carry a lovely memory of her with me.—HARRIET OSBURN, Lowell, Indiana.

(73)

If such a case, ending in such a way, could be a pleasure, certainly it was a pleasure to take care of Mrs. MacNair professionally. It has been my experience to meet few people with the natural charm which she possessed. I think we should all be everlastingly grateful that she did not have very much severe suffering. Frankly, I expected much more—in that we were fortunate. . . . .—DR. FLOYD F. PECKHAM, Chicago.

JUST BEFORE HER DEPARTURE
IT WAS WRITTEN

[APRIL 19, 1942.] There is nothing that can be said. I think I can understand in part what these last precious moments mean to you—and the waiting. And yet, except for us who love her and are to be left behind, I feel no sadness or reluctance—not for her, a spirit so vivid, so adventurous in the realms of knowledge and beauty. There could have been more years of earth's happiness for her, but I believe completely that here and elsewhere there is but one scheme, one endeavor, one goal: the enlargement of consciousness, and that is joy; the only joy. Hers will know its way into new ecstasies, and we could envy her the nearness of these if our minds were not now full of the realization that for a while we cannot share them with her, as we have done. Perhaps only for a little while, since it seems reasonable to suppose that threads which have harmonized in the part of the pattern we know may be brought together again for the same reasons in that part of the tapestry which is yet to be woven. . . . . .

Meanwhile, it is good of you to take time to let me know how things are. Give her my dearest love in those moments when she comes back from sleep. But do not trouble her with that if she is preoccupied. I know from experience of my own that the tremendous preparations the soul must make for its journey keep it preoccupied and remote, except at moments, from tendernesses it once welcomed. I know there is love in the atmosphere about her, and that is enough. MAUDE MEAGHER, Los Gatos, Calif.

PART IV

NOW SHE IS ONE WITH BEAUTY
(Composed in memory of Amy Lowell)
By ABBIE FARWELL BROWN

Now she is one with beauty. She who heard
The call of loveliness in each rare thing
Of craft or nature; lilacs, night of spring,
Feel of warm fur, old volumes crossed and blurred,
The subtlety of sound, the soul of a word;
Her firelit group in friendly loitering;
Great tragedy, quick humor; thoughts that sing
In the sweet passion of a bard or bird.

Now she is strong who faltered not in pain
From her beloved task; and joyous she
Who loved bright youth, eager and fleet again,
Companioned in a high felicity
"Among the Poets" whom she died to praise.
Now she is one with Beauty for all days.

SERVICE FOR FLORENCE AYSCOUGH MacNAIR

LARGHETTO	*Handel*
"ES IST EIN ROS ENTSPRUNGEN" . . .	*Brahms*
CHORALE IN E MAJOR	*Franck*
CHORAL PRELUDE	*Bach*

The Lord is my light and my salvation: whom shall I fear?
The Lord is the strength of my life: of whom shall I be afraid?

Organ response.

God is love; and every one that loveth is born of God and knoweth
   God.
God is light and in him is no darkness at all.
If we walk in the light, we have fellowship one with another.
He that loveth his brother abideth in the light.

Organ response.

Behold the Lord God will come with strong hand.
Behold his reward is with him and his work before him.
The Lord redeemeth the soul of his servants,
And none of them that trust in him shall be desolate.
They shall be abundantly satisfied with thy house.
For with thee is the fountain of light.
And in thy light shall we see light.

Organ response.

INVOCATION

Let us pray. Praise waiteth for thee, O God in Zion; and unto thee shall
the vow be performed; unto thee shall all flesh come. In this faith keep
us this day, that neither by day nor by night, in war or in peace, in life
or in death, may we pass beyond the bounds of that immortal being
that is thy life, who art over all and in all and through all, God blessed
forever. AMEN.

READINGS

I read from the One Hundred and Third Psalm.

Bless the Lord, O my soul; and all that is within me, bless his holy
   name.
Bless the Lord, O my soul, and forget not all his benefits:
Who forgiveth all thine iniquities; who healeth all thy diseases.

(77)

Who redeemeth thy life from destruction; who crowneth thee with lov-
ing-kindness and tender mercies;

Who satisfieth thy mouth with good things; so that thy youth is
renewed like the eagle's.

The Lord executeth righteousness and judgment for all that are op-
pressed.

The Lord is merciful and gracious, slow to anger, and plenteous in
mercy.

Like as a father pitieth his children, so the Lord pitieth them that fear
him.

For he knoweth our frame; he remembereth that we are dust.

As for man, his days are as grass: as a flower of the field, so he flour-
isheth.

For the wind passeth over it, and it is gone; and the place thereof shall
know it no more.

But the mercy of the Lord is from everlasting to everlasting upon them
that fear him, and his righteousness unto children's children;

To such as keep his covenant, and to those that remember his command-
ments to do them.

The Lord hath prepared his throne in the heavens; and his kingdom
ruleth over all.

Bless the Lord, ye his angels, that excel in strength, that do his com-
mandments, hearkening unto the voice of his word.

Bless ye the Lord, all ye his hosts; ye ministers of his that do his
pleasure.

Bless the Lord, all his works, in all places of his dominion: bless the
Lord, O my soul.

I read three short poems, translations of Mrs. MacNair's from
the Chinese.

Silent and alone, I ascended the West Cupola.
The moon was like a golden hook.
In the quiet, empty, inner courtyard, the coolness of early Autumn
enveloped the wu-t'ung tree.

❁

Scissors cannot cut this thing:
Unravelled, it joins again and clings.
It is the sorrow of separation,
And none other tastes to the heart like this.

He is going to the Tung T'ing Lake,
My friend whom I have loved so many years.
The Spring wind startles the willows
And they break into pale leaf.
I go with my friend
As far as the river-bank.

(78)

He is gone—
And my mind is filled and overflowing
With the things I did not say.

⚙

One could see, among the full, blowing clouds, the rocky sharpness of
peaks,
Were it not for the horizontal line of the Two-Edged Sword Mountains
cutting across the view.
They are flat against the green sky, and open in the middle to let the
sky through.
On their heights, the wind whistles awesomely in the pines; it booms in
great, long gusts; it clashes like the strings of a jade-stone psaltery;
it shouts on the clearness of a gale. . . . .
I bid good-bye to my devoted friend—Oh-h-h-h-h—now he leaves me.
When will he come again? Oh-h-h-h-h—When will he return to me? . . .
When the moon glistens on the Road of the Two-Edged Sword—Oh-
h-h-h-h—
I and you, even though in different provinces, may drink our wine op-
posite each other,
And listen to the talking
Of our hearts.

I read from the New Testament, the Beatitudes.

Blessed are the poor in spirit: for theirs is the kingdom of heaven.
Blessed are they that mourn: for they shall be comforted.
Blessed are the meek: for they shall inherit the earth.
Blessed are they which do hunger and thirst after righteousness: for
they shall be filled.
Blessed are the merciful: for they shall obtain mercy.
Blessed are the pure in heart: for they shall see God.

COLLECT

Let us pray. Almighty God, with whom do live the spirits of those who
depart hence in the Lord; and with whom the souls of the faithful, after
they are delivered from the burden of the flesh, are in joy and felicity;
we give thee hearty thanks for the good examples of all those thy
servants, who, having finished their course in faith, do now rest from
their labors. And we beseech thee that we, with all those who are departed in the true faith of thy holy name, may have our perfect consum-
mation and bliss in thy heavenly and everlasting glory. AMEN.

ADDRESS

You will not wish me to attempt a description of a life so many-sided
as that of our wondrous friend, so many-sided that any one of its phases
would be sufficient for the average life.

Many would be well content to have had the vivid experience of the
varied circumstances of her life. Born in China, educated in New

England, long resident in Shanghai in the beautiful Wild Goose Happiness House, she had a period of dwelling in Canada, another in the island of Guernsey, and lately in this present lovely House of the Wu-t'ung Trees. These circumstances included also traveling to and fro across all the seas and all the lands.

Many would have been well satisfied could they have made her record as a scholar, using the high intelligence that was hers for a great contribution to learning, as a distinguished sinologue and student of Chinese history and philosophy and art and letters.

Many would be well content if they might have achieved her success as a sociable person who loved company, who loved people, who numbered innumerable fellow human beings as her friends and still many more as her acquaintances. She was hospitable, always a sweet and gracious person through the days of many years in many places. A distinguished artist spoke of her as a "scholar, musician, artist and poet, but most of all a gracious woman, her enthusiasm for life makes radiant all who come her way."

She was the author of many books, works of scholarship most of them, but perhaps still more, works of high artistry and beauty. *The Autobiography of a Chinese Dog* has the charm of a work of art. *Firecracker Land* is delightful. Her translations of numerous Chinese poets, including the works of Tu Fu, were published [in part] in collaboration with Miss Amy Lowell. Add to these the rich *Chinese Mirror* and the stimulating, beautiful *Chinese Women*. All these works were based upon her own extraordinary apprehension of everything beautiful whether of nature or of art. Her love of trees and flowers, gardens and beautiful houses, was patent to all. Her collection of treasured objects of Chinese art, works of exquisite taste and workmanship and beauty, someone has said to be the finest such collection privately held in all the United States. Perhaps it is in this guise that she is best and most widely known, as an aesthete, a lover of beauty and a creator of beauty.

But she was a great humanist, and that in many senses. In the sense of humanitarian works, works of personal generosity, such as hurrying down this street to catch up with an agent whom in her preoccupation she had, so she thought, too abruptly turned away. This generosity was expressed in these last three or four years by an almost entire absorption in the works of China Relief in the midst of these terrible days. A humanist also in the deeper sense of personal friendship. Always she received the love of her servants because she gave them sincerity, honorable respect, and friendship. She was constantly helping students, perhaps not so much physically and financially as personally. Some of these I have met; many others could say what this letter from one of them[1] so well testifies:

"We are greatly shocked to know that Mrs. MacNair has passed

[1] Charles Y. Hu.

away. Our grief is so deep and we are so overstricken by this sad news that we do not know what to say at this juncture. To us, Mrs. MacNair has always been a kind, gentle, warmhearted, and generous person and has always been a great, sympathetic, and appreciative interpreter of our culture and our people to the Western world. Our country and our people have indeed owed her a great unpayable debt. . . . . Not only we estranged [exiled] students, young men and young women from China who are now here in this country, have been denied a guiding light and a vital source of comfort and inspiration; our country and our people have lost a great friend. . . . . It is indeed an irreparable loss to us all. We deeply deplore this sad blow befallen upon us at this critical time. . . . ."

No one knows how many have said in their hearts the same thing. Still more deeply, she was a humanist in the sense of her quick love of common human activities and her understanding of them. Her warm sympathy, her genius for comprehending folklore and folk customs, her desire to penetrate through things that were done by the people she knew, enabled her to look upon certain ancient customs not as crude or dark but as revealing lovely depths of life-experience, or marking simple deeds and necessities of human living with color and warmth and charm. For example, when she built her house [the Grass Hut by the Yellow Reach, in Shanghai], over and over again, some ceremony had to be enacted, some rite had to be performed, in the laying of the walls or the fashioning of timbers or other details. She followed these rites and rules with meticulous care because she saw in them something dignified and lovely. For instance again, at the annual occasion of the burning of the kitchen god, who keeps watch over the household members and who journeys each year to report of their manners and morals, her fancy and her warm quick realization of the meaning of this rite for the friendly servants in her household led her one year to have constructed a paper airplane so that the god might go quickly to the heavenly heights and hence more quickly return. Such whimsy, such gaiety, but such deep respect! For instance again, she once said that she could not live in Santa Fe because she had no time left to undertake the studies of the people necessary to make possible any true dwelling among them. Lastly, a great humanist she was, in the sense of being not wholly engrossed in the high culture of the beautiful, in the high romance of elevated letters or distinguished society, but as being practical, provident, energetic, simple, responsible, persevering, and competent in the ordinary necessities of life relative to the business or domestic aspects of living. To my thought, in all of these meanings she was, far beyond most of us, a great humanist.

Of her life-philosophy none of us knows very much. She had, I am sure, a strong intellectual sympathy and a considerable accord with the great ideas that are to be found in Chinese cosmogony, Chinese philosophy of the nature of existence. I know this because it was the subject of my first conversation with her. Some thoughts of my own she found to be similar to the ideals of some Chinese philosophers as set forth in her beautiful book *A Chinese Mirror*, in my copy of which she wrote the quotation, "Only Heaven is all seeing, all hearing and perfect in comprehension." In her life-philosophy she was not simply religious in general but practical and concrete. Though she saw reality and value in many faiths, here in Chicago she became an active member of this Unitarian Church to make her religion specific, and not leave it wandering loose in the clouds. You may be surprised to know that in this connection the thoughts that she most commended were not those of philosophical or artistic or whimsical or poetical character, but those that were the boldest expressions of the need for human justice and for experimentation in things economic.

How, then, shall we summarize this life, so quick in apprehension, so vital in energy, so warm in generosity? Perhaps to say that she was one of the greatest friends that China ever had; perhaps to say that she was one of a very few persons giving to the Western world intimate pictures that help us to comprehend this great and gifted people. I see her not wholly confined to any place, for the poetic name she used here and which was given to her in China long ago was "Love Poetry Sojourner." I see her not confined to any time but moving in a dark-blue Chinese robe of silk, embroidered in green and gold, amongst the learned assemblies, talking eagerly and intently with students and friends, walking in the garden of bamboos long ago beside the Hall of Mercy and Sympathy. I know that in these recent days, as she lived here with us, the bird of happiness did lodge in the branches beside the House of the Wu-t'ung Trees. I feel strongly also that already before her mortal life was closed she had passed through the great moon gate on the edge of the far, far west where it joins the east in that timeless place where dwell the people of the kingdom of immortal flowers.

PRAYER

Let us pray. O Lord, thou hast been our dwelling place in all generations. Before the mountains were brought forth, or ever thou hadst formed the earth and the world, even from everlasting to everlasting, thou art God. Thou art our home. Here we have no continuing city. Thy life is the abode of our spirits, in thy presence is eternal joy. By thy light may we see and understand and follow justice and right, and by thy spirit our minds and our natures are turned to the light and joy that is found in earthly places and in heavenly kingdoms wherever is manifest the love of the beautiful and the good.

We praise thee this day and thank thee for this gracious life to whose heart and mind were revealed so much of the wonder of living, so much that is beautiful, as she penetrated with seeing eyes many secrets of nature and of simple people, of laws and customs, of high and intricate thoughts, of nations and governments and races. We rejoice in her gifts

(82)

and in the generous heart to spread them bountifully through the world for the enlightenment of the human spirit, for the coming of larger days of freedom and happiness to the people of the world. Especially we thank thee for the long devotion to that people amongst whom her lot was cast and to whom she became an honored and beloved friend. We rejoice in her moving words helping us to see and to know them, helping them to become nobler in stature and valiant in spirit in their struggle for righteousness and peace in the earth.

Now may thy countenance be our strength and stay here and thy perpetual light shine upon her as she has passed beyond the mortal life of suffering and of joy to be for us evermore in a region of purity and peace, serene and holy, the dwelling of eternal truth and good, where are cherished the essences of brave spirits dear to us, become immortal in the worships and devotions of our own hearts. AMEN.

SENTENCES as the Urn was carried into the Sacristy

As she has borne the image of the earthy, so also she bears the image of the heavenly.
Then shall the dust return to the earth as it was: and the spirit shall return unto God who gave it.

BENEDICTION

May the peace of God which passeth all understanding keep our hearts and minds in the knowledge of God evermore. AMEN.

Sonatine from "God's Time is Best"   .   .   *Bach*

THE REVEREND DR. VON OGDEN VOGT

FIRST UNITARIAN CHURCH
CHICAGO, ILLINOIS
Monday, April 27, 1942, 3:30 P.M.

OF THE SERVICE IT WAS WRITTEN

ALL your arrangements are beautiful. Of course Anna [Monroe] and I went to the service, and we had good seats though they were not with your Mother. I liked the simplicity of the service and her colors in the chancel. I am glad you told me about the Sung vase, as I could not see it well enough to tell just what it was. I could not hear the words that were uttered, but Anna was deeply touched by them and said they were beautiful. You were fortunate to have a companion on that dark journey to Boston—and you can cherish the memory of a lovely place for her. I think so often of her beautiful deep eyes.—LUCY CALHOUN.

It was a relief to go into a church not loaded with flowers, and it seems to me that a service after cremation is the only one with dignity of spirit.—LUCY DRISCOLL.

It was a privilege to know her, and as we look back, a great inspiration. The service at the church was so beautiful—so perfect—one came away feeling uplifted—to try to do in one's small way—to make life more beautiful—as Mrs. MacNair has done so magnificently.—EMILY BISSELL.

There never was a more generous-hearted person, woman to her fingertips. I am so glad you had purple and red for her colors at the end. She glowed with life and loveliness. What a beautiful service you must have had! I wish I could have been there. Like you, I feel our "dead" are not dead at all, but spirit living in spirit. . . . . I looked up to her so greatly: so kind, so brilliant, so brave. . . . .

There really was never anyone like her: so warm and generous, so completely unselfish and true and loyal. . . . . I feel Florence opened Chinese poetry to me in a way nobody else could. Her books are such books of beauty!—DOROTHEA HOSIE, Taunton, England.

(84)

We had realized the extraordinary distinction of her personal gifts and graces, and we felt the reality of Dr. Vogt's tribute to her fine life. She seemed to us always a great lady in the best imaginable sense of that expression.—JOHN T. McNEILL.

The service was so simple and genuinely lovely, and the tribute paid Mrs. MacNair's influence and personality was as nearly adequate as human understanding and appreciation could make it.—BERNICE LANSBERRY.

FROM "PENUMBRA"

By Amy Lowell[1]

Sitting here in the Summer night,
I think of my death.
What will it be like for you then? . . . .

The old house will guard you,
As I have done.
Its walls and rooms will hold you,
And I shall whisper my thoughts and fancies
As always,
From the pages of my books.

You will sit here, some quiet Summer night,
Listening to the puffing trains,
But you will not be lonely,
For these things are a part of me.
And my love will go on speaking to you
Through the chairs, and the tables, and the pictures,
As it does now through my voice,
And the quick, necessary touch of my hand.

[1] From *Pictures of the Floating World* (New York, 1919), pp. 95–97. Inclosed in a letter from Helen Ely Griffin, Seattle.

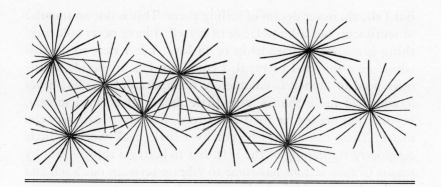

PART V

AFTER HER RELEASE

[MAY 13, 1942.] It makes me warmly, deeply happy to know that I am to have Ai's opals, to wear as she wore them and to love for her sake. No, I am not superstitious about opals. On the contrary, they are the only jewel I have ever cared for for myself, although I like to look at the colors of precious stones on other people. I have never worn any other jewel than opals, but I have not owned any since those I had in a necklace and rings were stolen in Berlin in 1920. Since then I have not worn anything of the kind. Now I will wear Ai's—*always*, and I will see to it that after I have gone, they will go only to someone who knew and loved her and will love them for her sake as I do. I adored them on her. I never see her in my mind's eye but with the opals at ears and throat. Strangely—no, not strangely, but so like her—I dreamed of her clearly and quietly last night, and when I found your letter in the box this morning it was as though she had come beforehand to quiet my mind for your description of her going from this place.

Again, how like her, the note in her memorandum: "If she does not care to wear opals she may sell them." There was an exquisite delicacy about her generosity, always. She wanted one to do as one might wish, never trying to bind one by obligation.[1]

---

[1] Nor, it may be added, did F. A. M. ever expect "gratitude" from a recipient of aid. Once I remarked to her, "*Well, he* should have been filled with gratitude for what you did." To which she replied, "Ah, my dear, *never* expect gratitude from anyone."

But I should never dream of selling them. This is not an impulse of sentiment, but a knowledge of myself. I have never sold anything given me in friendship or in love. I feel that to do this would be a spiritual betrayal. I could not face it. Beside it, the mere need of money is completely unimportant. Besides, never having had more than a very little money at a time, money, beyond that needed for food and a roof, has never been very *real* to me. These can always be got by a little hack work, a little temporary tightening of the belt. But to betray a thing—that by reason of associations has come to vibrate between one's self and another—one couldn't do it.

She felt that way I know—darling, darling Ai. I know the things she wore, and why she wore them. The [purple-and-scarlet] coverlet I made to tuck around her feet! It nearly broke me down when I read where you had placed it.[2] You must keep it please. It is yours. Wrap it around some of her things if you will, or burn it some day in the Chinese fashion with a thought for me to her, where she is.

Only yesterday in unpacking a cedar chest, I came upon the scarlet-and-purple afghan I have been knitting her for years. First it was to be a Christmas gift, then a wedding gift, then successive Christmases I hoped to get it finished. But I am a slow and laborious knitter (how quick she was at that!), and it is hardly four feet square yet, and I am out of wool again. If you want it, you shall have it as it is, dropped stitches and all. There is much love for her in it, but I should have known I am no good at that kind of thing.

It was good of you to write of the final things. And thank G.S. for me, if you will. And, please, will you tell me of anything I can do? . . . . The [Casa de Tierra] house [of *World Youth*] is full of memories of Ai, even though she did not see it. The gate to

[2] It covered the small table in the chancel on which rested the T'ang or Sung dynasty dull-red and brown pottery Urn during the service in the First Unitarian Church. The coverlet and the afghan are now in the F. A. M. Memorial Room at the home of *World Youth* (a magazine founded and edited by Maude Meagher and managed by Caroline Smiley, in which F. A. M. was deeply interested, and on the Board of which she served from the date of its founding until April 24, 1942), on El Quito Road, Los Gatos, California. In the Memorial Room, and in other parts of the Casa de Tierra, are the scarlet and gold lacquered Chinese bedroom furniture which came to the House of the Wu-t'ung Trees in 1936 from F. A.'s bedroom in The Grass Hut, Shanghai.

the inner patio, you know, is named for her, because she was, for me, the gate into an inner fulfilment. I am so glad she had you these last years. I remember very well the look in her eyes when she came back from China on her way to Guernsey. I knew what had happened, though it was long afterward that her telegram put it into words.

MAUDE MEAGHER

LOS GATOS, CALIFORNIA

DIARY ENTRY (TRANSLATED FROM THE CHINESE) FOR MAY 7, 1942

By HAN YU-SHAN[1]

AI SHIH K'E[2] born in Shanghai
Transcended world of Money and Extravagance Sea
Devotion for ancient culture
Diligence in search of its riches
Transmitting knowledge—not to
    flatter common taste
    in order to gain popularity—
But for real joys of kindred souls.
Her Knowledge and Life a Great Unity.
Reverently I burn "heart incense"
    as expression of appreciation
    and prayers.
Year of the Horse: Moon of Pomegranate: 7th Day
Han Yu-shan reverently recorded.

[1] Formerly a member of the faculty of St. John's University, Shanghai, Professor Han is now a faculty member of the University of California at Los Angeles.

[2] Transliteration for Chinese characters for Ayscough: meaning "Love Poetry Mother" or "Love Poetry Sojourner."

FLORENCE AYSCOUGH MacNAIR

By MAUDE MEAGHER

ONE knows that she is gone, but only deeper into that joyous and enchanting world created by her spirit here. Those of us who knew her have lost a dear and fructifying companionship: we cannot grudge a loss that brings to her new beauties, new enchantments. For these she will find. She found them here in all the changes of this earthly light, and she will find them, too, in the changing lights of other, lovelier worlds—because she took them with her.

She gave me once a gold pencil, already christened in Chinese "The Little Horse." This was in Guernsey, in the Channel Isles. As we walked together along the cliffs, above the sea, the little horse went galloping: a cloud with the snout and curved blue horns of a dragon; a cove where a mermaid loved a fisherman and died. We saw the mermaid's face in the rock.

In the Grass Hut in Shanghai one heard at all times the flutter of the Love Pheasant. There could be felt the presence of those birds that have but one wing each, and so may fly only together. She was, like every human, both Yin and Yang, but in her the Yin—inspirer of the Yang, the dark core at the center of the flame—burned deep and strong. Amy Lowell, Lucille Douglass, I, too, and how many others! felt the unsuspected buds of new creation swell in the warm darkness of her indulgence.

How shall I speak of her indulgence, her clear happiness when a thought had taken form. It touched and intensified everything —the spotted red toadstool and the luck-bringing chimneysweep tied to a cart outside Vienna; the three-legged frog that lives in the moon, found crudely modeled of clay in a Chinese village fair. I remember a strangeness in the light one evening in her London house, as she read aloud some newly translated verses of Tu Fu. There was a greenness as of under the sea—the sea from which the earth rose. Those tall flowers that I call the Flaming

Crane burned blue and yellow, and, as she read, the mountain peaks of China moved by in the thought of the scholar Tu Fu.

This was the Yin in her. The Yang everyone knows—her books, her lectures, her laughter, her scholarship. These are the light-giving edges of her flame. It is the light-inspiring center that we who knew her well especially remember, with gratitude and love. Sometime again, dear and lovely spirit, in some region of intenser light, new beauty, yet more ardent life!

FLORENCE AYSCOUGH MacNAIR[1]

By KATE BREWSTER

BEYOND a certain age, friends are not easily made, enthusiasms not easily aroused. I had reached that age before I knew Florence Ayscough, to us in Chicago, Florence MacNair. I hope and believe she became my friend; certainly I was hers.

Kind and wise, gentle and incisive, charming and straightforward, philosophical and simple, she seemed to embody all qualities of heart and mind which make woman delightful and potent.

"The fragrance of her deeds wafts down a thousand years." This is her translation of the eulogy upon a Chinese lady of very ancient days, and it might well have been written of her. Both her deeds and her words were fragrant, and what she said was amusing, expressive, and thoughtful, but never pretentious. Her great gifts were modestly borne.

To hear her quiet, sweet voice read the poetry which she had transformed so beautifully and intelligently from one idiom to another was to hear music.

The American Friends of China, and all other groups of which she was a part, will never forget her. Another phrase of her translations is fitly used:

"Can the one word 'grief' express all?"

[1] Prepared for, and read at, a meeting of the American Friends of China, Chicago, April 29, 1942.

FROM AMBASSADOR HU

CHICAGO

April 30, 1942

MY DEAR PROFESSOR MacNAIR:

I was greatly shocked and saddened yesterday afternoon when I was told of the death of your beloved wife.

Permit me to express my most heartfelt sympathy on your great loss in which China, too, sustains the loss of a great friend and interpreter.

I passed through Chicago twice before this. On both occasions I inquired about Mrs. MacNair's illness, but I did not wish to trouble you by telephoning.

I told a meeting of the Friends of China yesterday that, in her lifelong devotion to the interpretation of Chinese poetry to the West, Mrs. MacNair's systematic translation of Tu Fu was probably her greatest contribution to the Occident's knowledge of China. Tu Fu is the most beloved poet of my people—and considered by all the greatest poet of all periods of Chinese literature. But, because Tu Fu sang of the real life and suffering of the people, especially after the War of 755, he never found much favor in the hands of superficial students of Chinese poetry who only understood, or only were interested in, the "little" poems of love, wine, and dreaming of the lesser poets. Mrs. MacNair's introduction of Tu Fu and Waley's of Po Chu-i have been the most important efforts in popularizing the great poets in the English language.

Please forgive this lengthy note and please do not trouble to answer it.

With kindest regards,
Sincerely yours,
HU SHIH

REMINISCENCES

By Ella Potter Ely

THE noon swims in St. John's University gym—one summer, when I was working over the next year's plans and methods for teaching eleven classes weekly . . . .—were intense joy to me. All the others had departed, and we two had the pool to ourselves. I recall that while down at deep end one morning I said something about the universality of art which Florence did not think was true. She was standing at shallow end and I at deep. Forgetting where I was, I got my hand up to be more emphatic, and she saw me go down!!! We had a grand laugh when I sputtered up and hung onto the side of the pool!

The next day came her chauffeur with some great tomes of Chinese art, illustrated, which were simply wonderful to me. . . . . Just like her to help—immediate—

I confess I allowed her erudite reputation to hinder me in my chance meetings with her—I am so woefully ignorant of things Chinese—and to a great extent poetry had to be read *to* me, as she could read it, before I thoroughly enjoyed it.

Some of my happiest memories of Shanghai are those lovely afternoon reads with her in her lovely room, with the bookcases and fire making it all a dream come true.

Remember when she came down to our house on campus one time [to read Amy Lowell's "Guns as Keys and the Great Gate Swings"]? She brought her doggie, who sat in his purple-lined basket and looked quite as intelligent as her listeners. We had a standing-up tea after the reading. And did Florence stay with the nonmissionary group? Not a bit of it—out she went to the porch through the dining-room windows to seek the people she knew knew something—the "mishes"! You and Donald [Roberts] had a chat with her—I see you all three so clearly. . . . .

What a gifted person Florence was. . . . . Her languages—so proficient—her diction so good, and yet with it all so humble— a real sign of a great mind.

How well I remember the morning we got down to the hotel lobby in Vienna to see her off for a lecture tour into Germany, etc. She had on one of the most charming dresses that morning—made by the dressmaker[1] she allowed me to use. I know, when I saw her dresses, I wondered what the dressmaker was going to charge me for my things! But to my relief they were quite reasonable. I paid the bills with a sigh of relief!! More than likely Florence told them we were but "mishes"? I always shall feel so eternally grateful to her for coming to my assistance and seeing that I got some clothes that were warm as well as pretty. Until then, I never had connected Florence Ayscough as in any way enamored of clothes—thought she was far above them, though always she did look so beautifully gowned. I must have thought dresses just grew on her! Instead she was a keen observer and a wise and discriminating chooser. . . . .

All this past year in Honolulu as I studied Chinese art I found myself wondering if I might not write her and get her clear-eyed opinion on it.

Always she fascinated me. . . . .

I am so glad to have as my last memory the day she came down to the Medhurst Apartment and gave our Poetry Group such a glad morning that we were fairly carried away with her joy—and her personality. I am grateful for that—very. I found myself thinking as she read, and again when she chatted at the luncheon —that she was brimming over with joy, a joy I never felt in her when she was alone in Shanghai.

[1] Tillie Klopfer, a *friend* greatly admired by F. A. M.

CHERISHED MEMORIES

By Eva W. Dunlap

IN THE immediately post-revolutionary days of 1912, in Shanghai, the warm violin tone of Florence Ayscough gave forth a rich sincerity. Then, as later, she opened her beautiful home that those who wished might partake with her of the cultural satisfaction so astonishingly close at hand. A chosen group it was, but, though a stranger there, one might share the enriching growth—the things of the spirit which, like a sheltering tree, spread onward and upward throughout life. For though one cannot now hear her friendly eager voice, human and sympathetic with the simplest toiler, it yet speaks through the printed word, and one's children may recapture in her books the springs of their China happiness in days which have changed to something quite different.

In the spring of 1916, Mrs. Charles S. Lobingier asked a few friends to meet Eunice Tietjens, and Mrs. Ayscough was asked to speak of Miss Lowell as another contemporary poet.

"Of course, I cannot speak of Amy Lowell as a poet—but as a friend," and she lightly mentioned the long black cigars and the generous cables sent at Christmas and at other times. "When I demurred at the expense of these long cable-messages, she would say, 'But, my dear, why shouldn't I?' " The friendship of Florence Ayscough and Amy Lowell became a classic, and their charming letters are a delight and an inspiration.

When, after two years in America and nine years among the golden roofs and ghostly courtyards of Peking, we returned to Shanghai to live, I regretted a little that there the sun seemed to have so little of beauty and interest to shine upon!

"I should not regret too much," said my friend. "This is the old China—the Yangtze River basin. Peking is hardly mentioned in the old books." And, later, at tea in her charming house, built according to every tenet of Chinese custom—from the *Hei-yo-ho* of the pile-drivers to the exquisite ceremony arranged for the little Goddess of the Household—I realized that in Shanghai, indeed, lay the heart of an ancient Chinese culture. How clearly do I remember the moon fireplace with the stately Love Pheasant rubbing framed above it—a rubbing brought thence from a stone carving in Szechuen! Opposite on a table sat a bowl of eye-refreshing stones in clear water—for Chinese scholars to gaze upon—brought from Rain Flowers Hill in Nanking. Their round form and delicate colors refreshed all eyes.

But for inspiration—one turned to the hostess who served tea with such grace and who talked of this and that, stimulating one's interest in the timeless aspects of China's history, literature, and thought.

Once—because she herself had to be away—Florence Ayscough bequeathed to me the care of a visiting friend who was lame, and the memory of that act of friendship and courtesy became for me a joy for the rest of her mortal life and longer.

When the great Burlington Exhibition was in process of preparation in the spring of 1935, Messrs. Hobson, Eumorfopoulos, Sirén, and Sir Percival David came to Shanghai. One great day they attended a meeting of our Shanghai Art Club to hear Mr. James Plumer and to see his collection of T'ang and Sung potteries. But on this occasion I felt that it was the lovely personality of Florence Ayscough which cemented understanding and mutual delight.

Dr. Sirén had just finished his matchless study on Chinese art, *The Chinese on the Art of Painting: Translations and Comments*, and presented the contents of two of his chapters in the form of a lecture before the Royal Asiatic Society. Mrs. Ayscough had read through all of the manuscript[1] and, together, they had arrived upon that apt translation of *ch'i-yün sheng-tung:* spirit resonance and life movement. *Ch'i-yün* is the first and foundation

[1] Dr. Sirén's gracious acknowledgment, p. 6, of his Introduction, was as follows: "These [translations] would however have shown more shortcomings and inequalities, if it had not been for the kind assistance of Mrs. Florence Ayscough who during my stay in Shanghai, in February 1935, read through the whole manuscript and introduced a number of valuable suggestions and corrections. Her deep interest in Chinese thought and her experience as a translator became to me a support and an encouragement, for which I was under deep obligation."

principle of all Chinese painting and is mentioned over and over in Chinese art works.

And, now, the *ch'i-yün*—the spirit resonance—of Florence Ayscough, which came to dwell in the House of the Wu-t'ung Trees (since on wu-t'ung trees alone may the Bird of Happiness dwell), remains glowing and inspiring—remains to warm and encourage those who still reside in, and those who come to visit, the last of the homes which she made joyous, the home in which she was so happy—as Florence Ayscough MacNair.

FROM ONE WHO WAS IN "THE COTTAGE" AT ST. ANDREWS

By Nora Miller

She was so clever, and yet so humble, always trying to help people who really needed it and helping them in a way to help themselves and did so much good in a quiet way so that few people know just whom she did help and so many kindnesses with her thought—the kind of thing money could not do for them. . . . :

. . . . for our Lovely Lady did so much good here. But she did it on the quiet, and few people—but those it was done for, and my husband and self—knew anything about it, as she believed in helping individual cases instead of big institutions. If she could bring pleasure into a life, she did it. . . . .

She loved the country and its scenery here; with all the travel she had done, she thought it prettier here than anywhere else. That is why I was always looking for her to come back for a visit, but it wasn't to be.

I think I was the one in St. Andrews who missed her the most when she left. She was always doing some kind deed for me: a lift to St. Stephen, a ticket for a lecture, or a tea, or the loan of the car for a whole day before it was put away. Oh, well, we have the memory, and one can still feel the influence of having known someone worth while. I do so wish you could have had more years with her. . . . .

. . . . I just tell myself it is one's influence which goes on living, and it is the spirits of those who have been so wonderful in life who go on working for good after their bodies have left us . . . . and there are so many things she did for others that I'll have to write you again. . . . .

And do not be too lonely; she would not like it. Her idea in life was to try to give people the things in life which made happiness for them. The first thing she did for me was to make me have my little son with me. She asked the others first if they would object, because, she said, "If I can put any happiness into that life, I would like to." (She did not know that I had been very ill and that I was away because the doctor ordered me away, and I felt guilty. I was working unbeknown to my husband.) . . . .

She was real good and did things in a quiet way, not letting people know; she believed more in helping the individual than in doing something with a big show to it—for instance, the canon of our church (English) asked her to help raise money for the church, and she said, although she was not keen on lecturing, she would be only too glad to do it if it were of any help; this much she told me.

She did not believe in paying people's bills for them, which I think is quite right, although I heard that Mr. Ayscough went down and paid a grocery bill for a man before 10:00 A.M. one morning of $300 because they were going to jail him if it were not paid. No doubt she had a hand in it. The man was working part time for them, and they were paying him a very good wage. He was not worth it, and, after they had paid all that, he stuck out for a higher wage. . . . .

She believed more in helping people to help themselves. Just the same, I believe she footed any amount of bills but did not let on, as she had so much regard for their feelings. I know she put in a telephone in a house where they could not afford it, and there was sickness, and it was rather isolated. She thought that was practical; so it was, when you come to think it out.

But the thing I like to think of best is: I was having a birthday party for Joseph—I think he was six years old—and I asked them to come, and we were playing "Musical Chairs." I was handling the gramophone, and I had a piece on it that Mr. Ayscough thought wonderful (Jewish piece), and he wanted her to listen to it. He was sitting there enjoying it, but, like me, s'pose he didn't understand a word of it, but she smiled (I can see her now), and she went around with the children with Yo-fei in her arm (and he was fat and heavy), but she looked as if she had never enjoyed anything like it.

She gave Joseph a Christmas party on her twenty-fifth wedding anniversary, when she herself should have been having one. It was a wonderful time, and she made them all presents; besides the children, there were a few friends and people who had worked at the cottage in her brother's time or father's time.

Then another thing, which always stands out in my mind, is the treat she gave the high school. I can't remember if she had shown pictures or just Chinese articles, but she wanted to give them eats, and she wondered if sandwiches and cookies would be good. But I suggested fruit, especially oranges (they were hard to get at a reasonable price—for a few years here—60 cents a dozen the cheapest), and when she called me in to see the table, she had dishes of oranges, and buns, and pink and white peppermints in cellophane bags. It was the nicest table, I think, I have ever seen: a lovely lace cloth and crystal flowers; and the children filed from the drawing-room into the dining-room getting one of each goodie. They thought that was great. I thought it was lovely—and a lot of that kind of thing she did, but I guess I would be writing for the rest of my life if I put down everything. . . . .

IN THE DRAWING-ROOM AT ST. ANDREWS

The porcelain jar (Kang) at the left, one of a pair, was a gift from the Empress Dowager, Tzŭ Hsi. Now in the Art Institute, Chicago.

IN REMEMBRANCE OF FLORENCE
AYSCOUGH MacNAIR, Litt.D.[1]

By Maxwell Vesey

I cannot imagine anyone who met Florence Ayscough—for
that is the name by which she was known to New Brunswick
friends—ever forgetting her. Her personality was so vivid that
she remains in memory a clear-cut, glowing figure. One cannot
associate the thought of death with her. She is one of those
whose lives make us confident of "survival," for it is unthink-
able that such a spirit should be blotted out when the body it
inhabited for a few years has become untenable.

I think of Florence Ayscough as I saw her first in the Autumn
of 1923 when she came to talk on China to the Women's Canadian Club of St. Stephen; later as she bent over my library
table[2] writing her Chinese signature in *Fir-Flower Tablets*, the
collection of Chinese poems she collaborated with Amy Lowell
to produce; or, again, in the same room speaking on a day, close
to the one on which Miss Lowell died, of the sorrow she felt in
the loss of her almost lifelong friend; or, still again, of her in her
St. Andrews home, in her upstairs study looking out over Passamaquoddy Bay, to which she always referred as the "Bay of
Plentiful Fish," giving a Chinese twist to the Indian word; or
with gracious hospitality welcoming her guests and showing her
Chinese art treasures in the great living-room where an immense
plate-glass window brought the Bay of Plentiful Fish close and
gave an enchanting vista which included the striking silhouette
of her Island lying directly across that Bay.

Many friends in this town retain the same memories of the St.

[1] From the *Saint Croix Courier*, May 14, 1942.

[2] Elsewhere Mrs. Vesey wrote: "During the time she was at St. Andrews she came frequently to our home, and, as the drawing-room is large, she spoke frequently in it to different club groups. I thought her the most wonderful person I had ever met and still think
so. At that time I was not a writer, but she urged me to take it up. Since then I have, curiously enough, become one, doing a good deal of historical research. . . . . Always when
I see the outline of her island, I think of her, and of her wonderful aliveness."

Andrews home and of the . . . . cabinets with doors[3] carved into black lace and lined with [translucent mother-of-pearl], which, when floodlighted, became of an amazing beauty; of the flagged terrace outside and the garden in which she took such pleasure.

One remembers her characteristic dress and the colors, purple touched with scarlet, she made peculiarly her own, and the magnificent opals she wore so often. She comes into remembrance with her finely modeled face with its broad planes, and the sweep of black hair from her noble forehead, hair which showed a curious dusky purple sheen, her stately bearing and her gaiety, her keen relish for life in its highest aspects, and her intense interest in her surroundings.

This interest I personally experienced when she became fascinated with the history of the Passamaquoddy region and threw herself into the subject with a mental curiosity and an absorption which brought to life old figures whose stories had touched the Bay. . . . .

During those summers the Ayscoughs spent at St. Andrews in the nineteen-twenties they sailed almost daily in their yacht across the Bay to their Island where they had put up a camp. And there they cut trails through the woods to the top of the lion's head from which vantage point one looks out over wide sea- and landscapes.

When Lord and Lady Willingdon paid a visit to New Brunswick in 1927 the vice-regal pair were entertained at the Island. The fog was dense so they could not glimpse the scene in which their hostess so delighted. The little cove by the camp where they landed was named Willingdon Harbor in their honor. . . . .

So many from here know the Niger Reef Tea House at St. Andrews which Mrs. Ayscough built and presented to Passamaquoddy Chapter of the I.O.D.E. The walls were decorated with seascapes painted by Lucille Douglass when she visited her. Miss Douglass was illustrator of some of her books.

In my association with Florence Ayscough in those days I thought of her as the most fortunate person one could imagine. She had everything: a splendid physique and good looks, a life so

[3] From an old Chinese house in Soochow, China. Four doors from the same source were placed in 1936 in cabinets in the House of the Wu-t'ung Trees.

free and varied that she was constantly traveling from the Far East to America and Europe and back again to her Chinese home that was built on the ideas and ideals of China. She had wealth that enabled her to gratify each wish and to practise a widespread generosity, a mind so rich and understanding, so avid for knowledge and such great powers of concentration in its winning, all combined with that kindness of heart and gaiety of spirit that made her so intensely lovable and threw a glow over what in a less many-sided nature might have remained scholarship alone.

For Florence Wheelock Ayscough MacNair was a very great scholar, among the most noted of sinologues, known all over the world for her knowledge of China, and with so complete a comprehension of ancient Chinese thought and culture that it would almost seem as though she had been part of it always and forever. Could one believe in rebirth, it might well appear that she had indeed been of China in the past, a great lady there, perhaps an empress. For she had a royal spirit.

Florence Wheelock was born in Shanghai,[4] where her father, Thomas Wheelock, a native of New Brunswick, had extensive mercantile and shipping interests. Mrs. Wheelock was an American. Mr. Wheelock's sister was Mrs. Charles Gove of St. Andrews. After coming to a hotel for a time, he built the house up on the Algonquin hillside which was later to be his daughter's. Summer after summer the Wheelocks with a staff of Chinese servants came to St. Andrews.

It was naturally supposed that, living at an early age in China, Florence Wheelock learned the language. Owing to the prejudice against it, she was shut away from it as a child, and when she returned to live in Shanghai after her marriage, the prejudice still existed.

In any case, as she has said, "Chinese was supposed to be too difficult for people in their right minds to undertake." A missionary bishop[5] friend of her father's first interested her in the ideographs, and then she bought a Chinese dictionary. That little dictionary lay on her desk in her St. Andrews house and was in constant consultation as she worked on the writings which were later to win her so much praise.

[4] January 20, 1875.
[5] The Right Reverend Mark Napier Trollope, Anglican bishop of Korea, 1911-30.

She has said herself that not until 1907, when she was invited to become honorary librarian of the North China Branch of the Royal Asiatic Society, did she take up the study of the Chinese language seriously. She writes:

"The hours I spent among the somewhat dusty shelves at No. 5 Museum Road, Shanghai, I count among the happiest of my life. New roads, barely trodden paths, opened for me right and left; men long dead spoke through the written word, and women whose loveliness had vanished centuries before seemed to rise from between the faded book covers. But I realized that unless I learned to read Chinese characters I could make no appreciable advance in comprehension. From that moment my mind was made up. I engaged a teacher and began to work."

It was in 1889, when Florence was fourteen, that her parents left Shanghai and went to live in Boston that their children might be educated in the United States. It was during that period that her friendship with Amy Lowell began. In her early twenties Florence Wheelock returned to Shanghai and shortly afterwards married Francis Ayscough, an Englishman, who was connected with a large British importing house in that city.

She made numerous visits to America, and it was during one in 1917 when she had brought over a collection of Chinese paintings for exhibition that the idea of *Fir-Flower Tablets* originated. She had made some translations with which to describe the pictures in her lecture, and she asked her friend Miss Lowell to put these into more poetic form. . . . .

In [the winter and spring of 1926–] 1927 the Ayscoughs were in Shanghai during the revolution and fighting of that year. Fighting took place close to her "Grass Hut on the Yellow Reach," but sitting before her Moon Fireplace Mrs. Ayscough worked on undisturbed. She was fearless as well as kind, clever, and charming. . . . .

The time came when the Ayscoughs disposed of their St. Andrews properties and went abroad. Mr. Ayscough became incurably ill, and, following treatment in Vienna, they took up residence in the Channel Islands, where he died.

Some seven years ago, Mrs. Ayscough married Harley Farnsworth MacNair of the faculty of the University of Chicago, also an authority on China and its history and culture. After her

marriage, Dr. MacNair was at times a lecturer on Chinese literature, art, and culture at this university. She was given the degree
of Doctor of Literature by Acadia University. She lectured before
the Sorbonne and the Royal Geographical Society, and countless
universities, colleges, and clubs all over this continent and
Europe.

Born of Canadian-American stock, her associations British-
American, something in China reached out and touched her soul.
Surely Florence MacNair belonged to China.

FLORENCE AYSCOUGH MacNAIR, 1875–1942[1]

By Donald F. Lach

It is difficult to evaluate the writings of an individual who was at the same time an artist and a scholar. Most of us are highly satisfied to be recognized as one or the other. But while her "writing-brush was full of life's movement," Florence Ayscough MacNair believed and proved that sparkling creative effort can be successfully combined with less inspirational, but more meticulous, scholarship.

It is certain that she never thought of China and the Chinese as anything but home and friends. Her very early years were passed in Shanghai and Boston, cities in which she spent much of her life. In the American city she and Amy Lowell became childhood acquaintances—a relationship which portended much for the future. At the age of twenty-three, Florence Wheelock married Francis Ayscough, an Englishman, whose business took the young couple to Shanghai. It was not until some years after that she began by chance to study Chinese.

In 1907, after having been appointed Honorary Librarian of the North China Branch of the Royal Asiatic Society (NCBRAS), Mrs. Ayscough took up serious study of Chinese. Progress was slow at first under the direction of several uninspired tutors; progress later became more rapid and insight deeper under the able instruction of a Chinese scholar, Mr. Nung Chu, whom she so whimsically called by his English equivalent, Mr. Cultivator of Bamboos. What had at first been an amusing pastime became in the years prior to, and during, the first World War the consuming interest of her intellectual life.

In .... [1917], Mrs. Ayscough came to America with a large collection of Chinese paintings for exhibition. Much of her time was spent at Sevenels, Amy Lowell's home in Brookline, and it was

[1] Reprinted from *Notes on Far Eastern Studies in America*, No. 12 (spring, 1943), pp. 23–27. Washington, D.C.: Committees on Chinese and Japanese Studies, American Council of Learned Societies (1219 Sixteenth Street, N.W.).

during these days that their collaboration in the translation of Chinese poetry began. The "Written Pictures" in poetic form fascinated and challenged Miss Lowell. While Mrs. Ayscough translated and interpreted the characters, the poetess attempted to bring over the essence of the Chinese into English poetic form. The results of four years of co-operative effort appeared in 1921 in *Fir-Flower Tablets*, a small volume of Chinese poems in English verse.

In the Introduction to this first great undertaking, Mrs. Ayscough outlined her approach to the translation of Chinese poetry. Before the NCBRAS, she had the year before read a paper on "Chinese Poetry and Its Connotations." Here she makes plain the difficulties confronted by the translator in dealing with allusions to everyday scenes, proverbs, and traditions. *Fir-Flower Tablets* not only attempted to clarify Chinese allusions, but also brought forth a radical change in the method of translation itself. It was Mrs. Ayscough's unique idea to convey in translation the fine shades of meaning and lyric qualities of such greats as Li Tai-Po and Tu Fu. The intermingling in Chinese art and thought of calligraphy, poetry, and painting she sought to make plain by an analysis of characters, explaining their pictographic implications as well as their final and adopted forms. Miss Lowell based her versions of the poems on Mrs. Ayscough's copious notes.

The pitfalls in such an ambitious undertaking are apparent to laymen as well as to scholars. It is at this point, however, that Mrs. Ayscough proceeded with the acumen of the scholar and the imagination of the poet. Rare qualities these, and they were bound to stir up a hornet's nest of dissenting sinologues and irascible poets. Arthur Waley, the distinguished student of Chinese poetry, criticized Mrs. Ayscough roundly for her analytical approach, while Miss Lowell received rough handling by fellow-poets. Whether the criticisms were just or unfounded, the fact remains that the collaboration gave to the English-reading public a collection of accurately translated Chinese poems, marked by brilliant insight into Chinese life, and well adapted to the English eye and ear by one of the most outstanding women poets in modern times.

The collaborators in *Fir-Flower Tablets* planned after 1921 to render in their unique fashion translations of poems from Tu Fu, the great T'ang poet. Unfortunately, however, Amy Lowell died in 1925 before she had time to begin work on the "poet of suffering."

Mrs. Ayscough was meanwhile occupied in the early twenties in attempting to present in semipopular form a survey of certain intimate details of Chinese life and tradition. *A Chinese Mirror* was the product of much living and a great deal of studying in China and with the Chinese. She included in this charming series of essays a simplified outline of a series of addresses which had been presented to the Royal Asiatic Society at Shanghai. Wrapped around the scholarly portions of the work are exquisite word-pictures which depict scenes from the author's life and which illustrate magnificently the importance of tradition to everyday life in China. Her account of the ceremonies and customs observed in building her Chinese home (The Grass Hut by the Yellow Reach) gives direct insight into the great deference which she paid to custom and detail, a characteristic which gave her a genuine feeling for historical continuity and for the living relation of the past to the present.

After the death of Amy Lowell, Mrs. Ayscough decided to make the Tu Fu book her own. Since it was not possible for her to translate the Chinese poems into unrhymed English cadence, she decided to give a translation for each ideograph and its implications, adding the fewest possible English words which are customarily understood in the Chinese text. In rare instances she translated not only the character but what she called its "overtones" as well. The difficulty of deciding which characters retain their historical significance for the Chinese eye was perhaps the greatest point of conflict between Mrs. Ayscough and her fellow-sinologues. In this single instance the reader is struck by her mental agility, by her ability to distinguish between sinological pedantry and the more imaginative realm of literature, and by her sincere attempts to reconcile one with the other.

The Tu Fu study was organized as the autobiography of the Chinese poet. Its chronological arrangement was simplified by translating directly from the *Tu Shih Ching Ch'uan*, a twenty-volume edition of Tu Fu's works. The earlier of the Tu Fu volumes (1929) sketches the poet's career to 759, when he retired from office as magistrate. The second volume, published in 1934, continues and concludes his career. In the translations of the second volume it appears that Mrs. Ayscough adhered even more closely than she had in the first volume to direct translation of each ideograph; she added fewer explanatory conjunctions, prepositions, and articles. What remains is more intelligible and has in its literal meaning something of the original *Geist* of the poet.

Even while engaged in her arduous labors of translation, Mrs. Ayscough had time and energy to cultivate and enjoy active living. It is difficult to imagine a person more vitally interested in her environment and in those about her. Nothing is more typical of her imaginative and vibrant personality than her delightful *Autobiography of a Chinese Dog*—her dog whom she named after the great Sung warrior, Yo Fei. Nor could there be a clearer delineation of the various aspects of her own life in China than in the study of *Firecracker Land* which she wrote for the Junior Literary Guild. Children read the book with delight; their parents read it with delight and appreciation.

Mrs. Ayscough traveled around the world many times. She had homes on three continents: in Shanghai, in St. Andrews, New Brunswick, and on Guernsey in the Channel Islands. She lectured on China and Chinese poetry before learned groups in most of the world's great cities. Usually, her talks were illustrated with her own photographs or with artistically painted slides by [herself or by] Lucille Douglass, the well-known etcher, who had contributed etchings to *A Chinese Mirror*, to the *Autobiography of a Chinese Dog*, and to Volume II of *Tu Fu*.

After the death of Mr. Ayscough in 1933, she married two years later Harley Farnsworth MacNair, Professor of Far Eastern History and Institutions at the University of Chicago. Upon coming to the Midway, Mrs. MacNair at once became a part of Chicago's buoyant intellectual atmosphere. She and Mr. MacNair established a beautiful home close by the university which they called "The House of the Wu-t'ung Trees."

During these years, Mrs. MacNair produced a work which she had long anticipated—a study of *Chinese Women Yesterday and Today*. She was especially well qualified to write such a work in her dignified independence as a capable and gracious woman:

capable as attested by the fact that she was the only woman ever to be an honorary member of the NCBRAS (1920), and by her honorary Litt.D. (1923) from Acadia University; *gracious* as attested by all who knew her. The first part of *Chinese Women* is a study contrasting the position of women before the Revolution and since. The heroine of the book is Ch'iu Chin, the revolutionary of modern China who was executed by the Manchus in 1907. Mrs. MacNair translated freely from the *Ch'iu Chin Nü Chieh I Chi*, and her English renditions of Ch'iu Chin's poems reflect once again her singular ability for making Chinese poetry intelligible to English readers.

Chinese Women was the last, and in many ways the most penetrating, of her books. It seems to the present writer, however, that it was misnamed and more properly might have been called *Chinese Ladies*, for it deals only in a small degree with the women of the masses. In modern times the "emancipation" of the Chinese woman, whether for better or for worse, has been a most characteristic movement. Although Mrs. MacNair doubtless recognized this fact, it is a pity that she did not profit from her unparalleled opportunity to give the Western world a detailed and positive analysis of the woman's movement in contemporary China.

Although she would not have admitted it, Mrs. MacNair was not only a scholar, but a poet and creative artist as well. No translator makes good translations without giving a great deal of himself. More than most translators, Florence Ayscough MacNair braved the disparaging comments of a minority of occasionally irate sinologues and poets when she unhesitatingly placed one foot in each of their spheres and defied either group to remove her. She was convinced, and she convinced others, that scholarship and creative ability are not at opposite poles.

THE MOST IMPORTANT WORKS OF
FLORENCE AYSCOUGH MacNAIR

BOOKS

Friendly Books on Far Cathay (Being a Bibliography for the Student) and a Synopsis of Chinese History. Shanghai, 1921.

Fir-Flower Tablets. Poems translated from the Chinese. English versions by AMY LOWELL. Boston, 1921. (French translation by MAURICE THIÉRY, *Tablettes de fleur de sapin*. Paris, 1928.)

A Chinese Mirror, Being Reflections of the Reality behind Appearance. Boston, 1925.

The Autobiography of a Chinese Dog. New York, 1926.

Tu Fu, the Autobiography of a Chinese Poet, Vol. I: *712–759 A.D.* London, 1929; Vol. II: *759–770 A.D.* London, 1934. Vol. II carries the title: *Travels of a Chinese Poet, Tu Fu, Guest of Rivers and Lakes A.D. 712–770.* (KLÄRE WOLTERS translated from the first volume, "Zwei Gedichtzyklen von Tu Fu," *Ostasiastische Zeitschrift*, VI [1930], 236–40.)

Firecracker Land: Pictures of the Chinese World for Young Readers. New York, 1932.

Chinese Women Yesterday and Today. Boston, 1937.

Some Notes on Puto Shan. (Pamphlet.)

"Reminiscences of Amy Lowell" (MS.). (Quotations from this work are published by S. FOSTER DAMON, *Amy Lowell, a Chronicle with Extracts from Her Correspondence.* Boston, 1935.)

ARTICLES

"Shrines of History; Peak of the East—T'ai Shan," *Journal of the North China Branch of the Royal Asiatic Society*, XLVIII (1917), 57–70.

"Chinese Poetry and Its Connotations," *ibid.*, LI (1920), 99–134.

"Preliminary Notes on the Literary Background of the Great River," *ibid.*, LIV (1923), 129–49.

"The Chinese Idea of a Garden," *China Journal of Arts and Sciences*, 1923.

"Cult of the Ch'eng Huang Lao Yeh (Spiritual Magistrate of the City Walls and Moats)," *JNCBRAS*, IV (1924), 131–55.

"Amy Lowell and the Far East," *Bookman* (London), [LXIII] ([March], 1926), 107–9.

"The Symbolism of the Forbidden City, Peking," *JNCBRAS*, LXI (1930), 111–26.

"Guernsey Megaliths, Their Secrets Revealed by Night," *Report and Transactions of La Société Guernesiaise*, 1933, pp. 1–12. (Notes based on a paper delivered before the Congress of Pre- and Protohistoric Sciences at King's College, London, August, 1932.)

"An Uncommon Aspect of Han Sculpture: Figures from Nan-Yang," *Monumenta Serica*, Vol. IV (1939), Fasc. 1, pp. 334–44.

"Mi Yüan-Chang Writes Poems by Hsü Hun—A Hand Scroll. Mi Yüan-Chang shu Hsü shih chuan," *ibid.* (1940), Fasc. 2, pp. 627–37.

"China and Japan: Antithetical Ideologies," *Review of Politics*, III (1941), 306–18. (With H. F. MacNAIR.)

[To the above bibliography may be added:

Chinese Pictorial Art. By E. A. STREHLNEEK. Text compiled by FLORENCE WHEELOCK AYSCOUGH. Shanghai, 1914. Pp. 323. (Followed by "Supplement . . . . of Bronze, Ceramics, and Jade. . . . ." (Pp. 73.)

Catalogue of Chinese Paintings Ancient and Modern by Famous Masters: The Property of Mr. Liu Sung Fu. Compiled by FLORENCE WHEELOCK AYSCOUGH. [Shanghai, 1915?]

"Architecture" (pp. 33–34); "Art" (pp. 35–36); "Jewellery" (pp. 261–62); "Painting" (pp. 418–20); "Sculpture" (pp. 500–501); and "Symbolism" (pp. 537–38), in *The Encyclopaedia Sinica.* Edited by SAMUEL COULING, M.A. (Edin.). Shanghai: Kelly & Walsh, Ltd., ... 1917.

Syllabus of Lectures on Chinese Paintings Delivered by Florence Ayscough before the American Woman's Club, 3d April, 1917. Shanghai. (Pamphlet.)

"Chinese Painting," in *The Mentor.* New York, 1918.

Florence Ayscough and Amy Lowell: Correspondence of a Friendship. Edited by HARLEY FARNSWORTH MACNAIR. Chicago: University of Chicago Press, 1946.

"Calligraphy, Poetry, and Painting," in *China,* chap. xxi. Edited by HARLEY FARNSWORTH MACNAIR. ("United Nations Series.") Berkeley: University of California Press, 1946.]

[It is planned that a considerable collection of translations from the Chinese, both poetry and prose, left unpublished by F. A. M. at the time of her passing, shall be published.]

FLORENCE AYSCOUGH MacNAIR[1]

By LADY HOSIE

WHEN Florence Ayscough (née Wheelock) arrived . . . . as a young bride in Shanghai, she was in her very early twenties; and she soon decided that, since her life was to be cast in China, she would learn to speak Chinese and to read Chinese literature. . . . .

Florence Ayscough came of intellectual Unitarian stock, had been educated in Boston, and, to her, an appreciative study of Chinese was a natural and pleasurable duty. Most of the years she spent in China she had a Chinese teacher reading beside her. The North China Branch of the Royal Asiatic Society in Shanghai was in low water, and for years she worked hard and successfully at its rehabilitation, spending her energies and her money freely as its Honorary Librarian. Chinese art also, with its beauty and colour, became her delight.

Her first book, *Fir-Flower Tablets*, was a translation of poems from the Chinese, done in collaboration with Amy Lowell. Her next, *A Chinese Mirror*, was a thoughtful analysis of the foundations of the Chinese social and governmental structure, with special regard to the symbolism of the imperial palaces of Peking. Soon, however, her love of the Chinese poets reasserted itself, and she published [1929] her translations of the poems of *Tu Fu—Autobiography of a Chinese Poet*, Volume I, together with a biography of that poet as deduced from the study of his works; and this was followed in 1934 by her [Vol. II of *Tu Fu*] *Travels of a Chinese Poet*.

Her rendering of the ideographs was full of vivid imagery, and the modern archaeologist, with his more recent discoveries concerning the structure of the ideographs, might not always sub-

[1] Reprinted from the *Journal of the Royal Asiatic Society of Great Britain and Ireland with Which Is Incorporated The Society of Biblical Archaeology*, Parts 1 and 2 (1943), pp. 119–20. For lack of space, many other notices, and resolutions of sympathy adopted by organizations, are omitted.

scribe to her reading. But she did a great service to the public in America and England by her enthusiastic introduction of so great a poet as Tu Fu, till then unknown to them. At the same time, when lecturing, she managed to convey something of the chanting tone and rhythm of spoken Chinese verse—no mean task.

Other lighter books had much charm: *The Autobiography of a Chinese Dog . . . .* , and *Firecracker Land.* Her last work, *Chinese Women Yesterday and Today,* had as a theme the realization that the women leaders of the present time are but successors of a long line of capable, though secluded, Chinese women.

Of a gallant and warm personality, she welcomed and encouraged young writers. Speaking French and German fluently, she lectured before many learned societies, and had friends in every capital in Europe.

In 1935 she married Professor Harley Farnsworth MacNair, the historian, and their Chicago home was a centre of hospitality, open to all from the Far East. To her bereaved husband our sympathy is extended.

PART VI

ETERNALLY THINKING OF EACH OTHER

By Li T'ai-po

. . . . (*The Man Speaks*)
WE THINK of each other eternally.
My thoughts are at Ch'ang An.
The Autumn cricket chirps beside the railing of the Golden Well;
The light frost is chilly, chilly; the colour of the bamboo sleeping mat is cold.
The neglected lamp does not burn brightly. My thoughts seem broken off.
I roll up the long curtain and look at the moon—it is useless, I sigh continually.
The Beautiful, Flower-like One is as far from me as the distance of the clouds.
Above is the brilliant darkness of a high sky,
Below is the rippling surface of the clear water.
Heaven is far and the road to it is long; it is difficult for a man's soul to compass it in flight.
Even in a dream my spirit cannot cross the grievous barrier of hills.
We think of each other eternally.
My heart and my liver are snapped in two.

—Fir-Flower Tablets, pp. 89–90

ORIENTAL EXHIBITIONS[1]

By CHARLES FABENS KELLEY

Two special exhibitions in the Oriental Department will be of interest to museum visitors for the next few months. Both have been made possible through the generosity of Professor Harley Farnsworth MacNair, who has presented a large collection of Chinese *objets d'art* to the Art Institute in memory of his wife, Florence Ayscough MacNair.

In gallery H5 are some very handsome rubbings of the Ch'ing Dynasty, portraits, and birds and flowers. Those who saw the recent exhibition of Han rubbings[2] will marvel at the freedom and spirit of these later works.

Gallery H9 is devoted to the work of two dashing impressionistic painters of the nineteenth century who also specialized in birds and flowers. Those who have thought that Chinese painting was always formal may here find reason to revise their opinions. Indeed, conservative contemporaries are said to have considered the work of members of the Jên family as "being forceful beyond the limits of law."

Jên Po-nien (1839–95) was a native of Shan Yin near Shao Hsing, Chekiang Province, and his family was famous for its painters. During the nineteenth century he was considered very unorthodox, but now his work is greatly admired. It gives an impression of swift characterization and rapid execution. Only the big aspects of things interested him.

The monk Hsü Ku (1840–95), Jên's contemporary, shows many similar characteristics. His original family name is not

[1] Reprinted from the *Bulletin of the Art Institute of Chicago*, Part I, Vol. XXXVII, No. 4, p. 53.

[2] See *Bulletin of the Art Institute of Chicago*, Part I, Vol. XXXV, No. 7, pp. 114–16: ". . . . Dancing figures in the round may be found in a near-by case, and figures of similar type will be seen on many of the rubbings which line the wall cases. Most of these were made from sculptured tomb chapels from Nan-Yang in Honan province, and date from the first and second centuries A.D. They are lent [later presented] by Professor and Mrs. Harley Farnsworth MacNair, who acquired them on a recent trip to China. . . . ."

known, though he was a military official during the T'ai Ping rebellion. He is said to have been so sickened by the experiences of war that he turned to painting for relief. His monkish name means Valley of Emptiness, perhaps a reference to his state of disillusion. He was a wandering soul, traveling from Yang Chou to Su Chou and to Shanghai, spending many months as a guest in various cities where he painted until restlessness drove him on again.

THE FLORENCE AYSCOUGH MacNAIR CHINESE
COLLECTION IN THE LIBRARY
OF CONGRESS[1]

FLORENCE AYSCOUGH MACNAIR CHINESE COLLECTION. The [1,292] books in the Chinese language, comprising more than a hundred items, used by the late Florence Ayscough in her translations of Chinese poetry and in her writings on Chinese women, were presented by her husband, Professor Harley Farnsworth MacNair. Most of the volumes have in them the *ex libris* of both Professor and Mrs. MacNair, which bears a motto taken from the Confucian *Analects*, Book VII, Chapter 2, "Learning without satiety, Teaching without being weary." The collection contains, in addition to poetry, history and biography, works on drama and calligraphy in which Florence Ayscough was also interested.

[1] *The Library of Congress Quarterly Journal of Current Acquisitions Covering the Acquisitions of July, August, September, 1944*, Vol. II, No. 1 (November, 1944), p. 106. Published as a supplement to the *Annual Report of the Librarian of Congress*.

THE FLORENCE AYSCOUGH MacNAIR COLLECTION OF RUBBINGS IN THE UNIVERSITY OF CHICAGO

May 19, 1945

DEAR MR. MacNAIR:

On behalf of the University of Chicago Library, I have the honor to acknowledge your gift of 103 rubbings and six rolls of Chinese calligraphy in memory of your wife.

If it meets with your approval, we will keep the rolls and rubbings together as a collection in a portfolio marked, "The Gift of Harley F. MacNair in Memory of His Wife, Florence Ayscough MacNair."

I am deeply appreciative of this generous gift to the Far Eastern section of the library.

Yours sincerely,

RALPH A. BEALS
Director

THE FLORENCE AYSCOUGH MacNAIR MEMORIAL
ROOM IN THE CASA DE TIERRA
LOS GATOS, CALIFORNIA

May 19, 1946

WHAT a wonderful, wonderful gift to *World Youth* for a Memorial to our beloved Ai! The cases arrived two or three days ago, and we have been carefully unpacking them ourselves and bringing each lovely piece from the press-room (where the big packing cases were first put) up into the safety of my own room, which is next to the room we planned, when you were here, as the Memorial Room. This room has been cleared of its furniture —stripped down to the dark-red hand-made tiles of its floor, its white adobe walls, and the gold tea-chest paper of its ceiling. The drapes and bedspread were made from a hand-woven purple silk and gold sari that Caroline [Smiley] had, and we think Ai would have liked us to leave these, since they combine beautifully with her red lacquer things. The bronze knocker,[1] of course, has been for a long time on the door leading from the top of the patio into her Memorial Room. This door is wreathed with MOON flowers—so lovely and sweet-scented at night, and bordered on each side with Chinese forget-me-nots and white watsonias. This autumn there will be masses of red and gold chrysanthemums.

Just now we are in the throes of putting the wonderful bed together. I remembered, in a general way, how beautiful it was, but the beauty of its detail and color is a continual joy to us as we see it again. . . . . The desk arrived in perfect shape (with its exquisite ornaments) and so did the chair (except it needs some glue). What a beautiful set they are!

They stand temporarily in my room to leave us space in the Memorial Room for assembling the bed; and each time I look

---

[1] One of a pair of Ming Dynasty small dragons said to have come from the Forbidden City, purchased in Peking in 1939, and mounted to serve this purpose. The one mentioned here was on the door of the House of the Wu-t'ung Trees until it was sent to the Casa de Tierra. Its mate is now on the door of the House of the Wu-t'ung Trees.

at them I seem to see a dear figure seated there, deep in her beloved studies. It will be an inspiration to young visitors to know how she carried on with her chosen work in spite of distractions and a certain ignorant point of view among the socially minded that pidgin English is enough to get on with in China, and why study more?

When the Memorial Room is ready, I shall put into it the pictures I have of her, all her books, and her letters in letter file boxes, covered with gold tea-chest paper with her golden carp on the outside. I want to put your books there, too, and your letters, and a photograph, if you will let me have one, inscribed to *World Youth*'s Memorial Room. . . . .

Many, many, many thanks. You will come, won't you, when you can. I'll write you again when all this beauty you have sent to our Casa de Tierra—House of Earth—has been suitably arranged for Ai.

M. M.

NOTE BY H. F. M.

IN ADDITION to the above-mentioned Memorials, the following may also be listed:

In the Museum of the Chicago Historical Society: many pieces from F. A. M.'s wardrobe in the costume collection for the third and fourth decades of the twentieth century.

In Acadia University, Wolfville, Nova Scotia: several framed etchings by the late Lucille Douglass.

In The China Society, Inc., New York: the collection of slides, prepared by Lucille Douglass and F. A. M.—in memory of both artists.

In the Beloit College Museum: a collection of textiles.

In the Art Institute of Chicago: the pair of stone lion-dogs which at one time were in the front courtyard of The Grass Hut by the Yellow Reach, and which were later at the entrance to the House of the Wu-t'ung Trees.

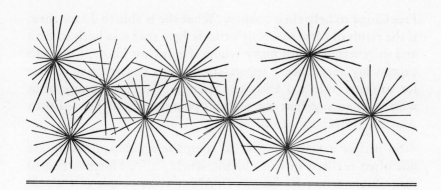

PART VII

If there be no affinity those face to face know each other not. If there be affinity those a thousand li *parted will meet.*[1]

AS SHE APPEARED TO A FEW OF HER FRIENDS
EXCERPTS FROM LETTERS

I CAN remember with such vividness that afternoon at your house, how charming, how vivacious, how quick with interest she was. Mrs. Abbot and I have frequently spoken of that delightful occasion—the tea, the conversation, and particularly the friendly understanding which was so immediately apparent. . . . .—C. D. ABBOT, Buffalo, N.Y.

I am one of a large number of persons who did not know Mrs. MacNair personally but who felt a deep sense of personal loss when the word came that she was gone. I have known for a long time of her great generosity and constructive kindness through some of our Chinese students to whom she was both very generous and very kind. These students thought of her as a friend, and they and others who will come in the long future will count her loss as a personal loss. I remember that Mrs. MacNair was wonderfully helpful to our Miss Wen-hsien Chen when her needs were serious and she did not know which way to turn. Miss Chen is now doing splendid work, training social workers in

[1] On a scrap of paper the Chinese characters for the above, with translations, in the handwriting of F. A. M. were found in one of her portfolios.

Free China to help their country. What she is able to do for them is the result of Mrs. MacNair's timely help that was both so kind and so generous. With many whom she did not know, I want to express my very sincere appreciation of her constructive service for so many able and friendless students. There are many of us who wish to say that the world is poorer without her.—EDITH ABBOTT, University of Chicago.

So perfect a marriage and so complete a companionship are not often realized in this chaotic world. . . . . Florence had so magnificent a zest for life. . . . . About some people one would say that it was better for them to leave a world torn asunder; but I feel sure Florence wanted to see through the struggle of China, England, America—all the countries she loved and understood. And certainly her understanding of both her adopted countries could have been useful to thousands of us now.—PAULA RELYEA ANDERSON, Westgate, Md.

This is not just a personal loss, for all of us who love China, Chinese literature, and Chinese art are deprived of a fine and understanding scholar in those domains. Your wife's profound knowledge of, and genuine enthusiasm about, all things Chinese has left an indelible stamp on the works she wrote, and those works will live on. . . . .—LUDWIG BACHHOFER, University of Chicago.

I so enjoyed the meeting we had in your home, for I felt there more thoroughly the Chinese atmosphere I so often enjoyed in many homes in the Orient. I was loath to leave that day; I just wanted to stay longer and quietly take it all in. Mrs. MacNair so charmingly seemed to fit into that atmosphere. I shall never forget that afternoon and your hospitality.—WILLIAM F. BARNES, Chicago.

It comforts me when I think of the long hours Florence must lie there, to know the beautiful world she can go into, because she has built it up through the years by her attitude toward life. Most people either drift or use their thought power wrongly. [Later:] Her spirit triumphed over everything. Neither of us can ever forget her lovely voice and smile. . . . . She will be with you always. "She has just stepped out into the invisible" as a friend of mine said of the person she cared for most, who had gone on the great adventure.—ADELA BARRETT, Chicago.

Her rare, lovely sensibility to the beauty and poetry of life, her generous response to the fulfilment of others' needs, make her live on in unnumbered hearts as a very warm and cherished friend.

The Chinese Ambassador yesterday spoke with such deep feeling and admiration of her at a meeting of the Friends of China.—FLORENCE DIBELL BARTLETT, Chicago.

Florence . . . . is *the* interpreter of China . . . . everything she wrote had a rare integrity and a flavor quite its own. . . . . No one has ever approached her interpretation of China, her integrity, her fine instinct for the quintessence of Chinese art and life. Tu Fu seems to me the *only* translation of Chinese poetry. . . . . Florence will be known to all lovers of China, as long as her pages exist.—DOROTHY GRAHAM BENNETT, New York City.

What I do know is goodness, delightfulness, and such unswerving honesty of idea, intent, and conviction that I am happy with her as I am with very few people. . . . . Indeed, it is very hard for me to think of her except as intent upon the thing which she is doing and possessing the purpose and energy with which to do it.—KATE BREWSTER, Chicago.

The first time I wore the scarf you gave me I had the same experience I did on only two other occasions in my life. . . . . On both these occasions it was as though I had received a benediction, and the influence of it has never entirely left me. It was exactly the same when I put on that scarf. Your wife was very vivid to me then—the tone of her voice, the expression in her eyes, the radiance of her personality, her sweet courtesy, her fine mind, and her unusual ability.—EDNA BILLER, Chicago, and Fort Smith, Ark.

Mrs. MacNair will be remembered not by her endearing mannerisms, the engaging little lilt with which she said "Goodbye," the way, when speaking, of hesitating to find the word with the precise meaning she wanted, then, eyes flashing, picking it out of the air—these were external pictures—but for the dignity of her soul before which one stood abashed by the pettiness of one's own character. Knowing her, one cannot but believe in immortality. . . . .

No one will ever know all the good that she has done. There was no patronage in her kindliness but rather a joy that out of her abundance she could share with those less privileged. How many lives are brighter because she passed that way!—FREDA W. BISHOP, Peoria.

She was unfailingly charming, and our PEN meetings will never be just the same without her. . . . .—FANNY BUTCHER BOKUM, Chicago.

She will long be remembered lovingly here where she made so many friends in so short a time. I have just sent a check to the China War Relief "in memory of Florence Ayscough MacNair, who taught me much of the beauty of China."—ANNIE WILSON BONNER, Chicago.

I remember so well those pleasant minutes I spent in your home with Mrs. MacNair and you. . . . . What a charming lady she was—and it pleased me so to see how you were together. . . . . Surely Dante knew what it all meant when he wrote that wonderful line—"E'n la sua voluntade e nostra pace." . . . . —GRAY C. BOYCE, Princeton, N.J.

I can imagine that she *is* cheerful—indeed, I believe you are right and detached in judgment when you say she is the most remarkable human being you have known—with her I have always had an awareness of qualities . . . . that makes me realize her stature—the stature that you know. . . . . Always in our minds is the memory of the evening in your home, when Florence read those poems in her lovely voice—I had heard her give them before, but that evening in your home, in your own background, your friends about you, had a very special quality. . . . . [Later:] We are all poorer for the loss of that rare spirit—I do not know when anyone has made so deep and lasting an impression on all who knew her.—MARY HASTINGS BRADLEY, Chicago.

Mrs. MacNair has symbolized to me one of the most beautiful aspects of Far Eastern studies. Her lively appreciation of the gracious aspects of life, Chinese life in particular, will remain impressed on my mind as one of my fondest memories.—WILLIAM BRAISTED, University of Chicago.

Her matter and manner were so delightful, and she spoke with such depth of knowledge. . . . . Once I asked her if she would give a lecture in my own home to raise funds for a church hall. She did so, and gave the first seven pounds, as the result of her lecture, toward the Hall which was subsequently built.—SIBYL BRISTOWE, Poetry Society, London.

That brightness can *never* fade. She has made a bright path for us all to follow as best we can. With her brilliant mind and broad sympathies and understanding she has made a place for herself in this hard old world of ours, and in our own small community, which makes us better and braver. . . . .—CLARINDA D. S. BUCK, Chicago.

I shall never forget her *radiant* face when I first saw her after your marriage. How great a joy it must be to you now to realize how happy she has been with you and how you have given meaning and joy to her life!—PEARL S. BUCK, Perkasie, Pa.

She was, we all felt, of such a rare quality that it was always a privilege just to meet her, to hear her beautiful voice, be greeted by the radiant sweetness of her smile.
Her remarkable attainments and unusual gifts were carried by her with simplicity and humility as became the lover of truth and beauty. How freely and unstintingly she gave from her richly endowed nature to all who came to her as to a fountainhead of wisdom and learning!—ROBERTA BURGESS, Chicago.

She had for me that poignant poetic quality that is so rare and can never be forgotten or obliterated by absence.—RUTH G. BUSH, Chicago.

I shall always be glad to remember the picture of her in her scarlet Chinese gown, standing before the big window in the library. She had dressed up to show the gown to Mercer. That is a fitting way to remember her, so characteristic and in keeping with her charm. . . . .—THOMAS BOWYER CAMPBELL, University of Notre Dame.

I recall many happy and pleasant meetings with Florence in different parts of the world, in London, New York, Shanghai, and once our paths crossed in Paris. Last week I had a letter from a friend who is serving in the Army, and who had recently come across *A Chinese Mirror*, and from a reading of it had been led to read Tu Fu's Autobiography in its two volumes which he had managed to obtain from a library. . . . . [He] was enthusiastic in his appreciation. . . . .

I shall always remember the support you and your wife gave to us when you were here at the outbreak of the war. The continuation of your stay here, and your unhurried going when it was finally necessary for you to leave, was heartening and reassuring. . . . .—JONATHAN CAPE, London.

I count the months and years that were enriched by the warmth of her friendship and affection as a special gift of the gods, and I shall always remember and be grateful. . . . .—ELLEN CARPENTER, Chicago.

It was she who opened my eyes to the beauties of Chinese art and literature and inspired me to an interest which has helped me through difficult and discouraging days. . . . .—ANN CARRÈRE, Havre de Grace, Md.[1]

She was such a wonderfully alive person, it is impossible to believe that such a life could come to an end. . . . .—DAGNY CARTER, Shanghai, and Claremont, Calif.

The passing of Mrs. Harley MacNair is a great loss not only to her family, but to our University community and to the whole city. For her bright personality, her interest in and knowledge of China, her gift for poetry—all her rich talents have been so generously shared with the rest of us, that it is a real sorrow to realize that such a colorful, inspiring friend has gone from our midst forever.

In the few years that she had lived here, she had made a very precious place for herself in our community, and it is very sad to lose her.—DOROTHY I. S. CHAMBERLIN, Chicago.

[1] One of the "Three After-After-After Travelers" on the Great River, China.

China lost a great friend. As the Chinese often say when they are in grief, "There is no place for a good person in this world." . . . .—H. T. Chu.

You know there are some people that you never can forget, and Mrs. MacNair was one who always seemed so close that I could almost touch her.—Elizabeth Claiborne, Shanghai, and Millersburg, Ky.

We—the members of the New Brunswick Branch of the Canadian Women's Press Club—remember with pride the part she took in making the Triennial in St. John an outstanding success.
It is the wish of the New Brunswick members that a resolution of sympathy be sent to you from our annual meeting. —Marian E. Cox, *Secretary.*

Your marriage was so ideal that, like your friends everywhere, we all seemed to share its richness. Six years of the character of your union were well worth while, far more than a quarter or half a century of the ordinary kind.—Earl Cranston, University of Redlands.

I wish that I might have seen her more, but I always felt that she was so generous with her time to so many people and things that she had the right to claim some of her time as her own. I am the loser. There was beauty and grace and understanding with her such as few people possess.
There are a great many nice people around to make life pleasant. I think you know Mrs. MacNair was more than that to me. With her there was fun with gentleness, gentleness with strength, and strength in a oneness with life itself. I could never forget her spirit, but the human in us likes the tangible. Something to see and feel and touch is comfortable. The warmth of a fire after having saturated one's inner self with the elements. . . . . There was so much of joy about Mrs. MacNair. To know her was to admire and to love and to laugh. In my thoughts of the cherished times I had with her I think of her showing me her kitchen devices and her own fun and mine in her description of the first experience with the pressure cooker and the noodles festooned on the ceiling. The graciousness and beauty of her very

(131)

being might become unreal in time but for her great humanness
—great because it could be so simple. . . . .—GEORGIA CRAVEN.

I had tremendous admiration for, almost awe of, Florence,
and yet she was so immensely human, so dynamic. . . . . What
a mind! You can imagine what an appeal that had for me. And
so she lives in all of us who knew and loved her. There is only a
little change.—ALEXANDRA DAVIDSON, Toronto.

She had an amazing talent for friendship and for making one
feel that she cared—and she certainly had an eternally youthful
spirit which is perhaps the greatest spiritual asset in life both
for one's self and for everyone else.—ELOISE DERBY, Boston.

Florence was so wonderful, so vivid, in her personality. . . . .
—EMILY DIMAN, Providence, R.I.

I remember Mrs. MacNair at that historical meeting in the
South [Chattanooga, Tenn.] about 1936 when she came to the
hotel room and filled it with all her charm and unique vitality.
Nothing, of course, can take away these memories from those
who knew her and loved her. . . . .—THOMAS E. ENNIS, University
of West Virginia.

. . . . One of the loveliest women I have ever known. . . . .
So few modern women know how to cultivate charm from within
as she did. . . . .
I was in her debt for all the wonder and romance which she
shared in her many inspiring lectures. She was generous in giving
two for our Woman's Club at the University Church of Disciples
—where the discriminating members agreed that hers were the
finest programs we had ever had in our club.—MIRIAM LIBBY
EVANS.

"Hail to thee, blithe spirit!" That line often came to my
mind when I used to see Mrs. MacNair. What a radiant, shining
spirit she was. She was like a bright-colored thread running
through the grayish fabric of University life—something
unique, exquisite, and irreplaceable.
And how eagerly and warmly she gave herself to all those she
met. The young boys at my fraternity house still talk about that
unforgettable evening when she read her Translations to them.

. . . . It must be a consolation to you to recall what a heritage of beauty she has left to so many people.—W. Nelson Fuqua.

So high-hearted and high-minded, so gifted and gracious, and distinguished in all the loveliest ways—that was Mrs. MacNair. And as we do truly "live by admiration, hope, and love," I am gratefully in debt to her for being what she was—an inspirer of all three. . . . .

She will always be like that

> . . . . lady sweet and kind,
> Was never face so pleased my mind.
> I did but see her passing by,
> And yet I love her till I die.
>
> —Agnes Gale, Chicago

One of the most lovely, unselfish women I have ever known has left us for a while.—Helen Gilbert, Chicago.

During the summer of 1938 it was my privilege to have the aid of Mrs. MacNair in the China Aid Council work that I was doing at that time. . . . . She sent me a Christmas card from China a few years back, which I still possess and cherish. . . . .

I met you in your home that summer at tea when I was planning with Mrs. MacNair an evening meeting in the "Chinese Temple" at which she gave us a talk on some of her experiences in China and showed beautiful illustrated slides. As I remember it, we raised several hundred dollars for the cause.—Stella Goldberg, Chicago.

I loved her dearly. Who wouldn't? One of God's own chosen. It can be truly said of her: she went about doing good.—Flora Grant, Fredericton, N.B.

I have a lovely memory of calling, a year or more ago, and found her coloring photographs [slides] in the great room, and the branches of the tree in your yard made a pattern in the east window—was that not the origin of your Christmas card? —Addie Hibbard Gregory, Chicago.

She was a *most* remarkable woman, so true, courageous, loyal, simple, and intelligent, as well as being completely self-forgetful. —Lisa Grierson, Boston.

Such a rare personality as Florence, whose many words and acts linger with us because of their kindness, penetrating wisdom, or playful humor. . . . . As I write, I have before me a beautiful flyleaf inscription which she wrote for me, and look out toward the "Heaven high hills" which she mentioned. —ELDON GRIFFIN, Seattle.

Of what I have read of her writing there was something which impressed me as so pure. Perhaps that is not the right word. . . . . Anyway I have a very distinct impression that the writer was a superior person, and there was a purity about it, the writing, which was quite unusual—also such a kindly touch. —ELIZABETH GRIFFIN, Pasadena, Calif.

We all feel so keenly, we who knew her, how indebted we are to her for many, many enrichments in our understanding of things beautiful. I loved her very much and shall always cherish the happy hours I had with her in your home and in the [Art] Institute. . . . . What a beautiful spirit shines out through all her erudition—she has left a valuable legacy to us *all*, and above all her own beautiful and penetrating mind to lead us into rich and ever lengthening pathways of knowledge and human understanding. She has seemed very near to me. And yet I love to think that she has soared on beyond this troubled world and now is among many of those great spirits she knew so well from a distance.—HELEN C. GUNSAULUS, Chicago.

Her light has long lit my path and will long continue to do so. . . . . I realize that I am only one of many whose lives she has touched and made happier for having known her. It is very wonderful to have so lived that one leaves a glow behind, one that will warm people for years to come. . . . . To have done what she has done is the ultimate goal of living.—LOUISE WALLACE HACKNEY, New York City.

She did *so* much to enrich all of our lives. Not only were her intellectual qualities a great stimulating force to her friends, but, even more, her spiritual outlook on life has been and will continue to be a real inspiration. I consider it a tremendous privilege to have known her. I always felt her outgoing-ness and warmth and her gracious mind.—EUNICE HALE, Winnetka, Ill.

What prodigious work your wife achieved. . . . . She had so much to instil into the New England's poet's mind. I feel always so privileged to have known her even slightly.—E. C. PRUYN HARRISON, New York City.

Each meeting is a strong and unforgettable portrait, and the books by her kept up our acquaintance. . . . . It was a lift and an inspiration to know her. . . . . And please do not think that I intrude when I say that I truly mourn that so happy a journey as you had together should come to its end.—AGNES LEE HASKELL, Kansas City, Mo.

Mrs. MacNair was one of those rare persons who unite scholarly thinking with genuine artistic feeling and a wide human outlook. It was always a stimulating and refreshing experience to meet her and to hear her talk. I shall never forget how kind both she and you were when I came fresh to this country four years ago, and the weeks I spent in your house will always be a pleasant recollection.—ROBERT VON HEINE-GELDERN, Vienna, and New York City.

Although I met Florence MacNair face to face for only a very brief time, I found her, at once, *muy simpática* and charming. Since then I have had frequent proof of her gracious thoughtfulness. . . . .—EDITH A. HILL, Redlands, Calif.

Florence had such an unspoilt, gay, cheerful, and lovely nature—ever young, hopeful, keen—and so refreshing and refreshed. She loved her friends—her own—and her work with such spontaneousness—and with such a pure love too. I shall always see her bright eyes, her constant alertness, and her "eagerness" in all she did or cared for.

I remember vividly the day she came to a prison for first offenders. I got her to wear those Chinese jades—and she lectured with lantern slides—and her whole manner and appearance and happy enjoyment of what she was doing—getting over to those men—until they really forgot their sad days—and responded—and asked questions and cheered her so spontaneously when she ended. . . . . I always felt with Florence that with all her permanent youthfulness of spirit—she *faced up* to things—then dealt with them—and then brushed their bad effects from herself. She bent her head when Fate was too strong—so was not broken—nor herself damaged. . . . . She knew nothing could really *hurt* her. She was singularly free within herself—and she combined that with such gentleness too. . . . . You must remember she had a very *happy* life—a full life—the life *she liked*, and did so many things she wanted to do—and that despite not being able to do such for years. But I think her "trials" only added joy to her triumphs, and her triumphs were great joys to her—and your coming to her was a wonderful thing in her life. —Helena Hirst, London.

I was thinking last night how Florence's life had touched every corner of the globe. She has lived richly and blessed all our lives. . . . . I cannot think of Florence except as being with us. Hers is a spirit that does not pass.—Alice Tisdale Hobart, Washington, D.C.

I hope something will be done to bring together her published works. . . . . We cannot have enough of such interpretations as hers always were.—Edward H. Hume, Changsha, and New York City.

Her personality was so vivid—and her gift for friendship so strong. . . . . Hers was a personality that can never be effaced—and I shall always have a lovely, vital memory of her.—Edith Jewell, Medfield, Mass.

The gracious personality of the lady . . . . elicited from the first our high admiration. We esteemed it a privilege to enjoy personal acquaintance with her, and she became associated in our minds with Nature's noblewomen. The influence of a spirit like hers is one of the things that make this world a better place in which to live. Mrs. MacNair leaves behind a memory that will be cherished by all who knew her.—Einar Joranson, University of Chicago.

To have known her only a very little and from a great distance has been a valued privilege to me. Out of my own experience I feel that in such a loss one can have no greater solace than to know that others have loved and been influenced by the one who had to leave us. . . . . So I venture to tell you that among the many many others who feel the same, I shall never forget her beauty, her charm, and the inner light that she radiated.—ELSIE FAY JORDAN, Chicago.

I remember with pleasure the evening I spent in your home when I was on the campus before; and the kindness of Mrs. MacNair in giving me a letter of introduction to Mrs. Calhoun in Peking. The Underwoods and Amendts have told me of their happy memories of your visit with them in Korea, and I know that Mrs. MacNair has brought much joy to uncounted others during her busy and purposeful life.—ROBERT A. KINNEY, University of Chicago.

. . . . her quality of intellectual pursuit, and whom I loved dearly for her sweet kindly neighborliness. I loved her acumen in gathering people together in your home for memorable teas and discussions, her sagacity and graciousness in making the Chinese as at home among her friends as though she were a spirit mistress within a temple. She taught me by her very living a new dimension of innerness which I know will grow stronger with the years. About a year ago now she brought me a lovely bouquet of tulips and iris from the garden; we always knew we had so much heart's room for each other. I have a packet of letters written on her exquisite stationery which I shall always keep. Would it bring you some moment of comfort to know that, one day coming home together from the Chicago Women's Club, I told her she was my answer to a lifetime prayer to be shown the useful and beautiful way of living. She squeezed my hand and smiled so understandingly. Your memory chain is exquisitely wrought, I know, and set with precious shrines. Through these experiences our horizons are extended on into the unknown, and infinity is brought within our touch.—MARGARET KLINEFETER, Chicago.

So great was her genius for friendship that one could feel as genuinely close to her at a distance, in miles, as when in her presence. There are few who have the happy ability to transcend space through sheer warmth and vitality of personality, and those few are the ones who can never be lost. Such keen appreciations of beauty and joy as hers could only be enlarged, never lessened.

Knowing Mrs. MacNair has been one of the genuinely fine things in my life. With Walt Whitman, "I no doubt deserve my enemies, but I don't believe I deserve my friends"—and I always had the feeling of not quite deserving Mrs. MacNair. Her friendship was one of those extra bonuses which life so generously gives us at times, of a currency which can be drawn on continuously, only to multiply and grow richer.—BERNICE LANSBERRY, [who took a course in Chinese Literature with F. A. M. at the University of Chicago].

She was very kind to us, and introduced us to Guernsey. . . . . We have *A Chinese Mirror* which she gave us, and into which I have placed a reproduction of W. Rothenstein's drawing of her. And I keep on my drawing-room mantelpiece the two Christmas cards sent us by her and yourself, with the representation of some of your Chinese treasures.—JOSEPHINE G. LEGGE, Oxford, England.

"Every noble life leaves the Fibre of itself interwoven forever, in the work of the world." Isn't it too true? and isn't it awfully true of what Florence left?—MARIAN LIDDELL, Shanghai, and Wheaton, Ill.

On those all too rare occasions when she was in New York and gave me the privilege of lunching with her, I always left her with admiration for her vibrant personality and appreciation of her powers of mind. One of the memories I treasure is of the day many years ago when she came into our office and read aloud to Mr. William Rose Benét and myself some of the Chinese poems she had translated with Amy Lowell, following her spirited rendering of the original Chinese with the English version.—AMY LOVEMAN, *Saturday Review of Literature*.

And I am so *glad* to know that the years Florence had with you were the best and warmest and fullest of *all* her life. That *is* rather a splendid thing to be able to think of about her. For she was rather a splendid person.

I am so glad you came that day, just before War began, to see us and she and Alice saw each other again and that A. and I met you, and I saw you and Florence together.—ANNIE MACLEOD, Brookmans Park, Herts, England.

She has been so kind and good toward us, so that we shall never forget the lovely hours we spent in her company. There are very few people in the world toward whom we have a feeling of confidence as we had toward her.—Gloria and Ulrich Middeldorf, University of Chicago.

No one I have ever met has been more wonderfully harmonious and enchanting in a deep way hard to explain. It so rarely happens that the body, voice, eyes—everything—are able to express the personality, the Spirit. . . . .

When I went to the Chinese exhibition, where we were so blessed as to hear her read those enchanting verses in her own translation, I saw, in one of the cases, an old bowl which was certainly the ancestor of some recent ones I had seen at Field's— so I bought two of them, and I am taking the liberty today of sending one of them, with some narcissus bulbs, to Mrs. Macnair. If you think best not to disturb her with such a little gift, please let them bloom in your home. . . . .—Anne George Millar, Evanston.

Delightful memories . . . . the soft glow of the jewel trees— the gentle shadows moving on your windows. And always, very clear and precious, the picture of Florence sewing in the library, the "black sheep" by her. Somehow, that little domestic scene just emphasized her many-sided interests and her real greatness. —Virginia Moncrieff, Chengtu, Szechuen.

She is such a wonderful woman, so lovely and gracious and understanding and with such a brilliant mind. . . . .—Anna Monroe, Chicago.

I find it hard to realize that a personality so vivid and a life so full of interest has passed from this world. . . . . Our earthly spheres were very far apart. I was just a poor country girl, but it never made any difference with either of us. We were friends from childhood.—Helen Mowat, St. Andrews, N.B.

For many years the Ayscough home in Shanghai was one of the few places where I could find an appreciation of the Chinese people sympathetic with my own—a real achievement for the hostess. . . . .

(139)

Later, in her own little house [The Grass Hut], with its charming Chinese atmosphere, I spent many delightful hours with the charmingly warmhearted, vigorously intelligent woman who was to become your wife.—HENRY KILLAM MURPHY, Shanghai, and Washington, D.C.

I have thought often of Florence these last months—before and after Pearl Harbor, before and after I knew she was ill—and of things she had said about the Orient. . . . . She was the first, and I think the only, person who told me that (whatever the intentions of the Germans) the Japanese really intended to conquer the world. How right she was. Oddly enough, I really never doubted that she was right.—JOHN U. NEF, University of Chicago.

I cannot feel Florence has left us, for her imperishable nobility will never forsake anyone who has made it a reality in their mind and heart. I can think of no woman more erudite than she, who gave her rich mind for the joy of others so freely. . . . .—KATHERINE OSBORNE, Boston.

The last time I saw her—which is the picture that remains in my mind's eye—she was so radiant looking that every one could not help noticing it. And besides that she kept saying, "Oh! I'm so happy!" and then laughing at herself, and then saying it again. Surely it must be the greatest comfort to you to know how much joy you bro't into her life.—MARIAN PEABODY, Milton, Mass.

I recall well the first time I had the opportunity of meeting Mrs. MacNair. It was at the meeting of Orientalists in Oxford in 1928. Though I never again had the pleasure of seeing her, I still retain clearly the memory of a rare and beautiful personality that reflected sensitively and with insight the whole view on life.—CYRUS H. PEAKE, Columbia University.

Her vivid outgoing personality, her beauty, and her music brought us together at once. . . . . I look at the line of her books and Amy's and what they did together—each with an inscription to me—and feel how rich I am in such friends and such memories.—ELIZABETH WARD PERKINS, Boston.

I looked up to her for her scholarship and I loved her for that rare spark of inner knowledge-and-delight she had in the field of intangible Chinese things. I had hoped for another visit with her in that marvelous library. It cannot be said in words. Believe me, I shall miss her much. . . . .—JAMES PLUMER, Ann Arbor, Mich.

She had an aura of the dignity and graciousness of Chinese culture, with large bits of the best of England and America added to her own individual charm, deep learning, and the glorious sense of the ridiculous. . . . . I loved her lectures from the first I heard . . . . it was on "Chinese Gardens." After that I went to every one I knew of, in cold or sunny weather.

She was an experience, an event, as you know, not just an episode. And always her dignity and graciousness! George and I already loved the Chinese; you and Florence have added much to that; you and they are part of our lives.

Florence was a unique and wonderful addition to the community, and her going away is a great, great loss.—JANE POLLOCK, Chicago.

I know countless others must feel this way, for Mrs. MacNair is loved by all who have known her. I think of her as a lovely and most gracious lady whose presence was for me always enriching.—BETSEY POSTON, Evanston, Ill.

Florence was one in a thousand for her wonderful personality and one that has enriched the lives of so many of us. . . . . What a privilege it was to know her.—EMILY G. POTT, Shanghai.

As you know, I regarded your dear wife with both admiration and affection, and when she asked me to address her as "Florence," I felt I had been taken in to the circle of genuine friendship. . . . . The relationship between Florence and you was an ideal one, and it will last to eternity.—FRANCIS LISTER HAWKS POTT, Shanghai.

I was with Mrs. MacNair not many times, but every one of these few occasions is attended in my memory with her warm kindliness. Especially shall I always recall an afternoon in your home when she was kind to my small daughter, over tea and cookies, and made my small daughter happy.—ROBERT REDFIELD, University of Chicago.

We have such need of all those whose souls are free of skin color prejudice. Not that such freedom from prejudice does any more than indicate the first thing your wife had to contribute to the postwar world we can hope for. All the sweet wisdom concerning things Chinese, the high values which were their high values!—ALICE WINTER REMER, Shanghai, and Ann Arbor, Mich.

I feel it was such a privilege to know her, to see the grace of the movement of her hands, and to hear her tell experiences from her great field of knowledge.—NAN RICE, Chicago.

I always regarded Mrs. MacNair as the finest woman I have ever known, and recall so many lovely and most helpful things she did for me and my school. . . . . When Acadia conferred the Degree of Dr. of Litt., she invited me to accompany her. . . . . It was one of the greatest pleasures of my life. Besides this I have so many other very happy memories of motor and water trips when she was a most delightful hostess.

While she was at her beautiful summer home she entertained my school many times. On one occasion she stayed until very near Christmas and gave them a real Christmas tree and treat. —ANNIE L. RICHARDSON, St. Andrews, N.B.

I shall always retain the most pleasant memories of Mrs. MacNair. I used to meet her almost every morning on her return from the walk with you to the Campus.—J. FRED RIPPY, University of Chicago.

You and Florence have been very much in my mind and heart these last days. And the fact that you are always together makes me realize what I've never felt so certainly before—that "togetherness" counts on so much more than the physical body.

As I think back on the years I've known Florence—the first time when Donald took me to see her just after we became engaged, up to the time we had together last month in the hospital —I wonder how any person can have united so finely *all* the qualities that one admires. Many people have a *few* things of

(142)

which their friends can be proud and in which they can take
joy. But is there anything in Florence which does not come in
that category? I doubt it. No one who has truly known Florence
as a friend is ever the same. He *has* to have a more gracious way
of life and a quickened perception of everything beautiful—because that is what Florence gave to her friends, and I believe
she goes on giving it, don't you?—FRANCES MARKLEY ROBERTS,
Shanghai, and Princeton, N.J.

I have so many memories of Florence—at Sevenels—we enjoyed the work so much. I was the "errand girl"—hunting the
libraries . . . . and after dinner, in the evening, such good talks.
. . . . What real fun we had.—ADA DWYER RUSSELL, Brookline,
Mass.

Florence was wonderfully gifted and many sided. The way she
took up the study of Chinese and also the way she threw herself
into the archeology of Guernsey during her confined sojourn
there were simply amazing. She was a dear little toddler of two
when I first knew her in the old days in Chefoo. . . . .—MRS.
SCOTT, Sundial Plain, Worplesdon, Surrey.

I venture, on behalf of the Council, to offer you our most
sincere sympathy in the great loss which you have sustained. We
feel that, with literature, we deplore the passing of a very distinguished writer and member of this Society.—[GENERAL SIR]
JOHN SHEA, Chairman, Royal Central Asian Society, London.

With what variety of qualities she was endowed! She possessed unusual intelligence combined with womanly modesty
and charm; she gave the impression of being a homemaker and
also one skilled in affairs. She had both creative and appreciative
gifts. She was idealistic, but not lacking in basic common sense.
As I recall her now, one quality stands out above all, and seems
best to sum up the effect on others of her personality: graciousness. How well she fitted in the gracious room, combining elements of East and West, which was her perfect setting.—SIDNEY
B. SNOW, Meadville Theological Seminary, Chicago.

Her vibrant personality was a real inspiration to all who knew
her. And she has given so much to the world. Surely her stay on

this limping old planet has left it enriched in many fields.—Amy S. K. States, Chicago, and Arcadia, Calif.

We feel as though a vital part of our lives had gone. Your deep happiness together gave joy and comfort to many of us. And she will never die in our thoughts—she is too real and strong and inspiring.—Jeannette and Jim Stein, Chicago.

What a fine, active life she led and how true were her words in my autograph album [quoted from her translation of Tu Fu]: "The work of my life can only cease when my coffin is closed." —Dick Steiner, Loudwater, England.

It is irreparable at this time when her rare knowledge and influence are so greatly needed. I count it an inestimable privilege to have known her.....—Marion Talbot, University of Chicago.

My first thought was "How pleased Aunt Nell will be to see Cousin Florence!" I can almost hear her welcome her to the new home. They have passed over the bridge to the better life.....Cousin Florence loved life and living for others; she gave so much of herself to others. I think her a wonderful person, and we feel it a great privilege to have known her. The pleasant memories she has left with us will be cherished the rest of our lives.....—Ethel Thompson, North East, Pa.

Only recently mother and I were talking of Mrs. MacNair, and we agreed then that she was our ideal of the very great lady. For to the happenstance of birth and breeding and rich gifts of the intellect, she added the crown of gentleness, generosity, graciousness, and understanding both wide and deep. She radiated those qualities, so that one was aware of them even in casual meetings. What they must have meant to those closest to her one can scarcely imagine, except that they were of such a high order that they must live on and comfort those she has left for a while. —Kate L. Turabian, University of Chicago.

She has made such a fine place for herself in the comparatively few years she had been here that her death is a real loss to the whole community. The memory of her as a gracious charming friend, always welcome among us, will linger on as a bright and happy part of our lives.—Russell Tyson, Chicago.

I am so glad I had those hours in your home on my short visit to Chicago. I felt closer to your wife then than I had ever before. We had such a pleasant talk together, just she and I, and she helped me to regain some self-confidence in a strange and unfamiliar world.—Eleanor Walker, Shanghai, and Great Barrington, Mass.

For me she has always been the ideal of a cultured woman and fine spirit, and I mourn for her as such.—Lili J. Warndof, Vienna, and New York City.

A rare and exquisite soul. . . . . I've known Florence since 1917—a long time. I shall miss her very much. We loved so many of the same things. It seems so wrong that a person so sweet and brilliant and good, with such a joy in living, should have to leave the world. . . . .—Florance Waterbury, New York City.[1]

Florence just by being did more to make Chicago a memorable experience for us than did most people by trying. I have known few persons so alive, so filled with the enthusiasm of one who loved to be alive, so captivating with her personal charm, so steadily the center of loveliness. Her whole personality seemed keyed to beauty, and she had the capacity for surrounding herself with an atmosphere of beauty. We shall miss her, for she was one of the few who make us homesick for Chicago. Something very lovely has gone out of our lives.

Yet she hasn't gone out of our lives, Harley. She remains among the memories which comfort us in the less happy times and in the uglier places . . . . memories of people and places and experiences which have enriched this earth for us. It might be added that Florence is the one "famous name" in my life who completely fulfilled my expectations. No other ever did in the same degree. . . . . And I choose to believe that, freed from the disabilities of the body, her lovely spirit has already found a

[1] In a letter dated January 7, 1927, after referring to the Chinese custom of burning paper models of utensils for use by the dead, F. A. remarked: "Florence Waterbury wrote truly when she said in a letter to me, the other day, 'In China the intangible is so tangible.' "

wider sphere of service, in which we shall one day join.—JAMES WATKINS IV, Ohio State University.

Considering what a sincere and helpful friend Mrs. MacNair had been to China and myself, I regard your bereavement as a personal loss as well as a loss to my country. . . . . Says Shelley:

> That garden sweet, that lady fair,
> And all sweet shapes and odours there,
> In truth have never passed away:
> 'Tis we, 'tis ours, are always changed; not they.

> For love, and beauty, and delight,
> There is no death nor change: their might
> Exceeds our organs, which endure
> No light, being themselves obscure.

On this view, I can conceive Mrs. MacNair as still living. . . . .
—HENRY WEI, University of Chicago.

No one has ever lived here so short a time and been so great a loss. She had so much to give and gave it so generously, and particularly those qualities in which Chicago is none too rich— her cultivation and scholarship enlivened with aesthetic appreciation—to say nothing of those qualities of which the world nowhere has enough—her breeding, gentle kindliness, and total lack of smallness. I hope she knew how much she was loved and appreciated.—HARRIET W. WELLING, Chicago.

One had only to meet her to realize what a wonderful personality she had—such a talent for making friends and never making others feel the superiority of her deep wisdom and knowledge. The Friends of China have lost a friend indeed and the whole city suffered a real loss. . . . .
I wish you could have been at the Friends of China meeting last Wednesday—there was such a spontaneous feeling of the deepest sorrow and regret about Mrs. MacNair. Then, when Dr. Hu [Shih] heard, he devoted the first half of his talk to Mrs. MacNair—how much he had enjoyed knowing her, and of her wonderful Chinese scholarship. He said that her translations of Tu Fu was a work of international importance which would endure.—FRANCES E. WHEDON, Lake Forest, Ill.

Dear Florence—I can't tell you how we, her oldest friends, loved her and admired her. . . . .—ELLEN S. WHITNEY, Milton, Mass.

We have lost for this life one of the choicest friends and the choicest lady in the world. . . . . Since she wrote me last summer about the grave of her great-grandfather [Rev. Pitt Clarke] in Norton, [Mass.,] and after I read about his devoted life, I have understood the life and works of Mrs. MacNair far better. She had to be earnest, even in a frivolous society: it was in her blood. So many facets to her character and life, and I know one. You know many, and your loss is that much greater.—MARY M. WILBUR, Shanghai.

Her character was a wonderful one, and I'm sure it must be a source of great satisfaction to you to know that during her months of illness you could be with her so much and shield her from much of the sadness. . . . .—ROGER J. WILLIAMS, University of Texas.

She was so gracious to me, so kindly and friendly despite the tenuous character of any claim I might have had upon her friendship, that I have been forever grateful to her.—FRANK G. WILLISTON, University of Washington.

The loss of Florence Ayscough MacNair is a grievous thing to endure—grievous for her friends and for the world. And it is a kind of comfort to know that some of her exquisite work was left behind so that we may have her "Last Translations" to look for.—KATHERINE WOODS, New York City.

I think especially of a luncheon . . . . one very hot day in August when Mrs. MacNair, in a most becoming costume, looked cool and won the admiration of all of us by her very stimulating conversation. Our entire city will mourn her loss! —HARRIET WALTON WOODWARD, Chicago.

PART VIII

WHEN THE LONG SHADOWS FALL
By F. L. MONTGOMERY

WHEN the long shadows fall to close my day
In which were golden morns of sheer delight
And flaming sunsets preluding the night,
Marking, as milestones mark, a traveler's way
Along which all the varied lights display
Their colors, gold, green, crimson to his sight,
Then may remembrance still continue bright
And through the falling shadows pierce their gray.

When the long shadows fall, though they conceal
The beauty of a world that I had known,
Then may I keep one memory for my own
That tongue or pen of mine dared not reveal;
So, sleeping, in my dreams I may recall
Her loveliness—when the long shadows fall.

"WE WILL KEEP OUR APPOINTMENT"
By Li T'ai-po

For a long time I shall be obliged to wander without intention;
But we will keep our appointment by the far-off Cloudy River.

> —From "Drinking Alone in the
> Moonlight," *Fir-Flower Tablets*, p. 39

THREE HUNDRED COPIES OF THIS BOOK

HAVE BEEN PRINTED

IN GARAMONT MONOTYPE

BY

THE UNIVERSITY OF CHICAGO PRESS

FOR THE AUTHOR

❀

THIS IS COPY NUMBER

75